MINDFULNESS AND TRADITIONAL CHINESE ZEN ARTS

The Way of Calligraphy, Painting, Kung Fu, and Tea

TRISTAN PETTS

Copyright © 2020 Tristan Petts

All rights reserved.

DAOSCAPE LTD is registered in England and Wales, United Kingdom.

Company number: 14463334

Address: 5 Brayford Square
London
E1 0SG

ISBN: 9781916078901

Cover design by Tristan Petts

www.Daoscape.com

For Anton

CONTENTS

	Acknowledgements	i
	Preface	iii
	Introduction	ix
1	Mindfulness and Zen	1
2	Yiquan Kung Fu: Resilience	43
3	Yiquan Kung Fu: Fluidity	63
4	Yiquan Kung Fu: Listening	79
5	Zen Calligraphy: Trace	87
6	Zen Calligraphy: Surrendering	93
7	Zen Calligraphy: Anchoring	101
8	Zen Ink Painting: Nature	109
9	Zen Ink Painting: Asymmetry	119
10	Zen Ink Painting: Mountains	133
11	The Way of Tea: Hygiene	141
12	The Way of Tea: Self	149
13	The Way of Tea: Flow	165
	Epilogue: Zen Arts as a Path	173
	Index	199
	About the Author	215

ACKNOWLEDGEMENTS

A big thank you to all of my teachers, especially Adrian Tuttiett, Mark Leonard, Wayne Bradbury, Dave Shepard, Uncle Wen, Jia Zhenzhen, Paul Wang, Jasmine Zhang, Patrizia Collard, Wang MingShan, Master Cui Ruibin, and the coaches and students at the Taolin International Yiquan Academy.

I also harbour deep gratitude towards friends along the Way – the likes of Anton Pick, Linus Lucas, Christopher Moreton, Andrew Barker, and A.J. Donnelly, who fueled my onwards momentum towards this book's destination during the most pivotal years.

However, greatest encouragement for writing and publishing this book has come from my father, who perhaps sowed most of the seeds that blossomed into the tree of wisdom that this work represents to me. It has been a great pleasure connecting with him more deeply over it all.

I am also indebted to my mother, as well as Jean B. Parr, for their editorial and formatting advice, and my sister, for cover design recommendations.

Lastly, a warm thank you to Wei MingPei for help with the Chinese elements, and to all those mindfulness and traditional Chinese culture fans – both western and Chinese, who have expressed vigorous enthusiasm for this project as and when it has been mentioned and discussed.

PREFACE

In my early twenties, I discovered a book titled *Zen in the Art of Archery*. It was written by a German academic, called Eugen Herrigel, who had studied the Japanese art of kyūdō (ritualised Shintō archery) between the years 1924 and 1929.

This exotic Zen-flavoured feat had been accomplished as a result of the opportunities Herrigel had enjoyed whilst teaching philosophy at Tohoku Imperial University, in Sendai, Japan.

His interest in Zen mysticism had been kindled much earlier than that, however – during his time studying theology in Germany. And so, in order to pursue further insights into Zen culture, Herrigel had decided to live in Japan.

Upon arriving in Sendai, he had discussed his deeper intentions with a local acquaintance he had made there, and was subsequently advised to take up a traditional Japanese Zen art – in order to approach Zen in a more practical way.

Soon afterwards, Herrigel discovered an eccentric kyūdō teacher and mystic, called Awa Kenzo, and began studying under him as a disciple – at the age of forty-one years old.

Around nineteen years later, in 1948, *Zen in the Art of Archery* was published in Europe – as a formal account of the German professor's experience when learning the 'Zen' of kyūdō for a few years in Japan.

The book became an instant classic in the West – especially as a gateway of sorts for lay readers to gain a glimpse of the Japanese Zen mindset.

And I also fell in love with that world of 'one shot Zen archery.' It kindled in me a strong urge to try to experience it all directly for myself, even – to follow in the German academic's footsteps, and become immersed in the magic and mystery of 'Zen kyūdō.'

However, not long after I had finished reading Herrigel's book, I encountered an article from the Japanese Journal of Religious Studies, titled *The Myth of Zen in the Art of Archery*, which was a highly critical account of the German academic's work.

Written by a Japanese author, called Shoji Yamada, the critique quite rigorously undermined the authenticity of various aspects of Herrigel's story.

For me, the most disappointing facts were that at the time of Herrigel's acquaintance with kyūdō in Japan, the formal art was not, and apparently had not ever been, a traditional Japanese Zen art or practice, and it did not even look to Zen teachings for useful insights.

For Herrigel's archery teacher, Awa Kenzo, was apparently more of a folk mystic than a Zen teacher during the German's period of study under him, with Awa expressing no absolute conviction in Zen philosophy or practice at that time. He also did not teach archery in a way that continued any kind of formal Zen lineage from the near or distant past.

The 'Zen teachings' that Herrigel purported to have received from his archery teacher seemed, therefore, to have been the result of a European Zen tourist attempting to match the Japanese cultural exercises he had practiced (as part of what was arguably more of a traditional Shintō discipline) with the information about Zen philosophy that he had encountered in Germany – an understanding that he had accumulated before he had ever set foot in Japan, let alone held a Japanese bow or arrow.

This is not to suggest that there are not Zen lessons to be learned from formal kyūdō, or that one cannot improve one's kyūdō ability through adhering to Zen principles. The point being emphasised here, rather, is that one can probably learn and apply Zen ideas when practicing *any* discipline. And yet, doing so would not make that discipline into a formal 'Zen art,' of course.

As a result of these insights into Herrigel's work, I thus began to become highly skeptical of purported Zen arts in general. Because, ultimately, any student of a discipline could assert that there is a formal Zen approach to, say, motorcycle maintenance, when in truth there is no classical or formally recognised lineage originating from Zen temples or ancient teachers that supports any such claim.

And this situation distressed me quite a bit, because I felt that I had already become enamoured with the ideals that Zen seemed to point towards, and I wanted to tune into the spirit of an authentic Zen discipline in order to get to know its true nature more intimately.

I eventually decided to go in search of the more true Zen arts myself, therefore – and not even in Japan. I chose, instead, to go to the nation from which all East Asian Zen arts emerged – namely, China.

For as history can tell us, the Japanese inherited all of their Zen teachings and disciplines from the Chinese.

After searching fruitlessly for authentic Zen arts teachers in China, however, I almost gave up at one point and decided to go to Japan after all. And yet, through a rather sudden and dramatic turn of events, eventually I did discover what I had been looking for in China.

That was more than eight years ago, and although I had no great intention to write a book on the topic of the true classical Zen arts of the Far East after only half a decade of formal acquaintance with them (no matter that period of time being longer than the time Herrigel had spent studying kyūdō in Japan), it was apparently my fate to experience, late one evening in Beijing, a jarring road accident that would cause me to become hyper-aware of my fragile mortal condition – an accident that would show me how easily the benefits of my hard work in acquiring authentic Zen arts training could be lost.

For even though I had emerged relatively unscathed

from that accident, with only bruises and one broken toe – after having somersaulted head-first at high speed down an open highway, it seems that it was only by luck that I had avoided enduring any worse fate, as cars were hurtling over the 'crash site' only seconds later.

During the recovery period that followed, I was forced to remain immobile for long stretches of time. And as I sat at my desk in my Beijing apartment – within the clouds of the city's heavy pollution, as well as my post-accident 'funk' – ruminating upon how luckily unlucky I had been, an intense urgency arose within my being – an impulse to begin recording and sharing what wisdom I had already gathered. I thus began to write this book.

In order not to risk another premature exit from this world, however – this time through boring myself to death with any protracted waffling on, I decided to approach the task of writing down my insights as if I intended to read them myself every day – as a means of refreshing and re-focusing my mind as to what the essences were (as far as I had gathered) of the Zen arts that I had encountered and had been practicing.

This approach seems to have been quite fruitful, for as the chapters unfolded, and I re-read what I had composed, I began to increasingly enjoy and gain confidence in the endeavor.

So this is what you hold in your hands right now – a labour of urgent and heartfelt love that continues to bring me renewed zeal and optimism every time that I engage with it.

I thus hope that you can enjoy its content as much

as I have enjoyed creating, shaping, and re-reading it – over and over again, as you travel through and along your own life's twists, turns, and somersaults, and perhaps feel inspired to take up a traditional Zen art (or two) of your own – before this wondrous, fragile existence comes to its inevitable end.

T.P.

Beijing
August 2020

INTRODUCTION

A JOURNEY INTO ZEN ARTS

Among some of my earliest childhood memories are spectacular kung-fu-flavoured action scenes from the Japanese television series *Monkey Magic*.

The show was an adaptation of one of the 'four great classical novels of Chinese literature' – a story attributed to the sixteenth century author Wú Chéng'ēn (吴承恩), titled *Journey to the West* (*XīYóuJì* – 西遊記).

It was not only the high energy action in those portrayed scenes that made a big impression on me, however. For my father's re-actions to it all as we watched together as a family were also highly captivating – his expressions of joy and excitement in particular, as he engaged with the fantastical storylines.

I can even vividly recall him right now – standing on the rustic British country lane that led down to our house, as he attempted to spin a stick that he had been carrying in the same kung fu manner as that monkey king hero – bringing the magical martial motifs of that powerful warrior to life – to *real* life.

His playful spirit – partly his own, as well as being an aspect of that traditional Asian monkey king character, caused me to want to emulate such 'super monkey' behavior myself. And this channeling gained an even deeper personal momentum when my mother, who enjoyed studying horoscopes and birth charts from ancient cultures, told me that I had been delivered into this world during the Chinese year of the monkey, and with a full head of hair, no less!

That information sealed the deal, then – from that point onwards I would attempt to embody and channel an assumed monkey king spirit when playing with others – to the point of telling people that my middle name was 'Monkey,' even.

Over time, however, as *Monkey Magic* was no longer shown on television, and I was teased relentlessly by my peers for seeming to reduce myself to the level of a foolish monkey, I forgot my original inspiration that had impelled me to pursue that character's energy, and looked instead towards more mainstream role models.

I thus went through various phases of appropriating the heroic traits of sports stars, wealthy businessmen, military figures, and so on, until one day, when I was twelve years old, I discovered a book about ninjas in my local library.

I was instantly infatuated with those mysterious characters – perhaps because there was something inherently *Monkey Magic*-like about them – something mystical, martial, and East Asian. This time, however, humans were at the centre of the action, which made it all the more realistic and socially appropriate.

And so, as I eagerly studied the details of how those legendary Japanese 'stealth warriors' were alleged to have overcome adversity – by way of a mixture of refined skill and martial prowess, I began to dream of what it would be like to become a ninja myself.

Whenever an opportunity to further explore the world of ninjas and East Asian martial arts presented itself, therefore, I would eagerly seek out any additional information that could give me clues as to how to acquire more ninja-like abilities.

As a part of that process, I discovered Jackie Chan kung fu movies, Japanese 'manga' animations, as well as videos showing full contact fighting competitions – such as the Ultimate Fighting Championship (UFC), which was, and still is, a mixed martial arts (MMA) contest.

And it just so happened that, in September of 1994, a ninjitsu practitioner won a UFC title fight, which signalled to me that what I had been drawn towards held the potential to make dreams come true in the modern world – as much as it had done centuries earlier in the Far East.

At that time, the internet was only just becoming available to the public, though, and so I continued scouring libraries and bookshops for further insights into ninja culture.

Eventually, I came across another highly engaging book about ninjas, which revolved around the art of the ninja sword – 'silent kenjutsu.' And that book presented me with my first formal Buddhist meditation method – a mysterious chant that ninjas were alleged to have used in order to refine their powers.

In fact, it was a text called the *Heart Sutra* – the very teaching around which, unknown to me at that time, the epic tale *Journey to the West*, and thus the *Monkey Magic* TV series, revolved.

For in that classic Chinese story, one of the lead characters – a fictionalised version of a famous historical Buddhist monk, called XuánZàng, received the wisdom of the *Heart Sutra*.

Such a blessing enabled the monk, as well as his monkey king bodyguard, to pass a number of rigorous tests created by Guānyīn (the 'Goddess of Compassion') – to the point that both of them eventually arrived at buddhahood.

And this theme of using the *Heart Sutra* to overcome challenges was also present in my new ninja book, with the author explaining that one could dispel fear from one's heart by just chanting the words of the sutra.

What is more, the verses were written out in Japanese, followed by an English translation, and so I was tempted to try to recite them – in Japanese, even. But in the end its content and practical context were just too exotic and ambiguous for me to have any faith in.

Introduction

For I lacked access to any kind of 'ninja school' or teacher that could provide practical insights into the world that was being portrayed by the book – or by the *Heart Sutra* chant, for that matter.

And so, as a result, the intriguing mystery of ninjas, magical chants, and their roles in medieval Japanese culture began to fade out of my life somewhat – their legacy becoming more of an entertaining fantasy, rather than a signifier of any deeper practical wisdom that may have been lying within reach.

That being so, the apparent wisdom embedded within traditional East Asian martial arts in general still held an allure for me – to the extent that, at sixteen years of age, I began practicing the Korean martial art known as taekwondo, which I continued to enjoy whilst attending university.

Eventually, however, my enthusiasm for taekwondo waned in favour of other martial disciplines – such as traditional Chinese wingchun kung fu and tai chi, that were being taught on my university campus.

For these more complex fighting systems, in addition to integrating traditional medieval weapons such as swords and spears into their approaches – something which, for me, validated their practical martial origins, seemed to have a greater amount of cultural depth to them. They promote, for example, through their physical movements, and thus pure body language, fine traditional ancient philosophies that can be applied within one's life beyond martial settings.

I therefore began researching as intensively as I could into these two traditional Chinese martial arts' philosophical backgrounds. And it was during that period of inquiry that I began to find a certain mysterious word cropping up over and over again – the word 'Zen.'

So I shifted my research focus towards the history of Zen, and I discovered that, despite its traditional mystical connotations, in its simplest form Zen implies a unified state of body and mind – a flowing along in harmony with the true nature of our conscious biological existence, and thus our broader nature in general – an idea that I found deeply fascinating.

In order to gain a more tangible grasp on Zen's key properties, therefore, I decided to read some formal articles about it as a path in and of itself – as a way of being, and thus an embodied philosophy separated from martial arts practices.

And this decision would result in a small personal awakening for me, in fact. For it seemed that Zen doctrines promised to deliver a condition of being that I felt I had been seeking since before I could remember – some sense of a deeper reunification with the universe, and the potential to transcend or overcome any obstacle.

It was something that had been represented, perhaps, by the ninjas described in the books that had captivated me many years before, as well as by the monkey king character in *Monkey Magic*.

And so, as I continued to delve as deeply as I could into the mysteries of Zen culture, a theme began to appear that linked all of the East Asian martial arts that I had encountered together – namely, their intimate connection with Zen principles.

For if a warrior can flow along in fearless harmony with nature, it makes sense that he or she can sustain a finer control over their body, and therefore function more optimally during a battle.

Thus, traditional Chinese martial artists – especially Chinese military generals, purportedly sought to combine their martial exercises with Zen practices – so that they could become more confident, and therefore competent, when facing inevitable adversity.

And even though such an approach can make quite simple, logical sense when contemplated as a theory, it was not all so simple *in practice*, since it necessarily required gaining increasingly deeper insights into the truth of nature – something that was, and still is, no easy feat.

For a Zen practitioner has to somehow directly witness and merge – *flow along* – with the truth that all objects are reflections of one infinitely great nature – so that they may gain a deeply rooted, unshakeable faith in the idea that the death of any individual thing or person is merely an illusion – a cognitive error, and therefore not something to be feared.

No matter this considerable challenge, however, such a mode of being appealed to me a lot – both logically and spiritually. And so, from then on I was hooked – attached to the idea of achieving such a union with 'the absolute truth of nature.'

I thus began to obsessively discuss and contemplate this apparently exotic and intricate practical philosophy, and quickly started to 'stink of Zen,' as some teachers put it.

Later on, I would find out that this is the very opposite of what formal Zen practice is about. And yet, as part of that new 'Zen philosopher' identity that I had begun cultivating, I did also seek a more physical, tangible, practical manifestation of Zen philosophy through martial arts disciplines.

For when pursuing mastery of such arts, in order to truly make progress, one is forced to limit one's thinking – to transcend to the purely physical level, rather than merely contemplate forms through the manipulation of shallow symbols.

However, after gaining a basic competence in tai chi and wingchun kung fu, I had to accept that the authentic Zen origins and more subtle mechanics of these arts were lost within the mists of time.

Therefore, I continued to look for and read about other practical martial arts that were more explicitly meditation-oriented, so that I could at least find a lower-case variant – some 'zen,' within traditional East Asian fighting arts.

This dogged persistence eventually led to my discovering the existence of a rare martial art called 'natural intent pugilism' – or 'YìQuán' (意拳), to use the Chinese name.

It appeared to be a more recent distillation of a traditional Chinese calisthenics system, and yet it was also purported to be closer to the roots of ancient Zen kung fu than most other disciplines of the sort.

I thereupon set about looking for a teacher who could impart to me the essence of yiquan. And as if it were my destiny to become acquainted with the art, I found that there was a class taking place every week just down the road from where I lived – one of only a few in the whole country, in fact.

So I eagerly went along to try it out, and after a couple of deeply satisfying taster sessions, I reduced my wingchun self defence practice and began exploring a new zen martial arts path. For I felt that I had finally found a discipline that could meet my requirements – a physical, testable, logical system for bringing zen philosophy into my life.

And yet, yiquan was much more mentally and physically demanding than the other arts that I had encountered. For example, it required a practitioner to stand still whilst holding his or her spine straight for considerable periods of time. This was apparently necessary in order to allow martial ability to somehow manifest over the years as one practiced – via a gradual yet stable change towards a more resilient condition.

In all honesty, though, I was not sure exactly how that condition was going to arrive. And yet, the discipline did seem to provide my teacher, Mark Leonard, with an impressive competence at combative pushing and shoving exercises, as well as a highly tangible upright and warmhearted presence.

I was encouraged, therefore, to persist at yiquan – to endure the agonising boredom and physical pain of 'standing like a wooden post' (ZhànZhuāng – 站桩), with the hope of discovering a deeper potential within myself – some form of insight that could help me to become more like my teacher, and thus more resilient.

During the standing posture practice, my knees would hurt a lot, however, and I became worried that I might damage my body irreparably. So I looked online for any advice on such matters, and found reports from other western practitioners who had been told by their doctors to stop the exercise if their knee pain ever became too sharp and persistent.

As a result, my enthusiasm for yiquan and its teachings began to wane – as it had done for the other martial arts, for I assumed that it only suited a certain body type, or required some sort of special conditioning from a young age.

I did not let go of my dream to achieve mastery of Zen in general, though – to become, as one may read in ancient Chinese and Japanese texts, a wise old happy-go-lucky wanderer of the Earth. So my next stop was a Japanese Sōtō Zen meditation school, which was again located not far from where I lived.

There at the zendo I learned the basics of the art of zazen ('ZuòChán' in Chinese; literally, 'sitting Zen'), which I continued to practice by myself at home.

And this was to be a huge life-changer for me, for it brought the formal Zen doctrines that, up until that point, I had only been contemplating, into the fully practical domain.

What is more, it just so happened that at every seated Zen session we would chant the *Heart Sutra* in Japanese – using those exact same words that I had attempted to fathom within the pages of my ninja sword book more than six years before, and which were the key to the monk XuánZàng and the monkey king's final enlightenment in the classic medieval Chinese story *Journey to the West*.

However, when chanting the verses along with my fellow Zennists, I found it very difficult to maintain my energy throughout the whole of the ritual, whilst the session leader seemed to be able to accomplish the feat with ease.

As I persisted in the practice, though, I eventually experienced how, with its relentless rhythmic harmonious chiming, the chant would discipline and refine a person over time – perhaps in a similar manner to how a blacksmith's hammering shapes metal into a more useful object.

Thus, the more I practiced the chanting, the easier it became – to the point that it felt enjoyable, even. For in a way, it was like a kind of 'holy cure' for troubled spirits – it exorcised any toxic self-obsession, like a form of psychic surgery, which invigorated both my body and mind.

And yet, it seemed that there was not anything particularly deep or mystical involved in the whole process. Rather, the tempering of my spirits appeared to be simply the result of applying pressure to – exercising, my attentional skills and energy reserves – in the same way that any physically strenuous activity does.

Another reason could have been, however, that the sentences being intoned, and thus 'channeled,' communicated the mindset – the preserved thought stream, of a buddha – an Awakened One.

For it makes quite obvious sense that by flowing along in harmony with the 'mind stream' of a buddha, one's spirits will feel a catharsis – cleansed and nourished, and therefore lifted out from the dusty world of toxic self-obsession for a time – no matter whether the words conveying that mindset are making logical sense or not.

And equally cathartic for me was the practice of sitting in Zen meditation in the Japanese Sōtō tradition. Since even though it was again highly challenging, it was simultaneously all quite fine and agreeable in aesthetics and simplicity.

That being so, beautifully simple things are not *always* the most attractive to us, and the sitting could easily fill me with dread at times – since it had a very sharp edge to it – like a samurai sword, perhaps due to that specific Sōtō lineage having been carried from Japan to the West by Taisen Deshimaru, who was a descendant of a samurai family, and a keen kendo practitioner.

In this way, I began to see the true scale of the 'Zen mountain' that I had chosen to climb and embody. It was considerable indeed – it required the courage of a warrior, and yet somehow it appeared achievable nevertheless. Thus, my zeal for Zen practices was renewed, and I looked forward to attending the zendo as often as possible.

This fresh growth just happened to coincide with my graduating from university and entering the world of work, in fact. And so, as I began moving from one job to another in search of better pay and career opportunities – passing through various industries and offices occupied by colleagues of differing races, religions, sexual orientations, work backgrounds, and generations, I put my Zen practice to the test – investigating first-hand which traditional Zen approaches worked for me, and which ones seemed unsuitable for life in a modern cosmopolitan city.

That period was altogether a rather colourful experience – it was the standard 'rat race' within which one would live for the weekend release; namely, getting drunk on a Friday night, in between appreciating pay increases and promotions here and there – eventually being able to buy a house and settle down.

And once all of that had been achieved, the final stage would be to enjoy visits from grandchildren, a good pension, and hopefully a relatively swift and painless death.

It did not feel quite right for me at that period of my life, however. I felt, rather, that I was in danger of becoming trapped long-term in a vocation that was not particularly set up for a budding transcendentalist such as myself at that point – the person I thought I was, or wanted to be.

For I dreamed of living more contentedly and congruently in every fresh moment – not just when 'free' from the beady gaze of my office manager.

What is more, I wanted to try meditating on craggy mountains – to admire and contemplate 'cloud seas,' practice tai chi peacefully in a park every day, and follow in the geographical footsteps of the ancient eastern Zen sages.

Was that all too much to ask?

Now looking back on it, probably it was! But I felt very strongly – *positively*, that I did not want to be just another guy drowning his stress at a pub every evening, or at home with a bottle of wine. I also did not want to become a monk. Instead, I wanted to experience a 'regular' yet wholesome human life that involved creating and maintaining a family – something that many famous and high-achieving Zen practitioners had apparently managed to do just fine in the past.

In order to figure out a way to get closer to my ideal Zen lifestyle, then, I continued reading every reputable Zen book that I could get my hands on – to find clues or hints as to how I should pursue my own most appropriate modern and culturally localised 'Way' forward.

For even though attending my local zendo was a very useful and profoundly life-changing experience, in fact I was finding it increasingly difficult to be sure as to whether that system had been appropriately installed in Europe, let alone the United Kingdom.

I began to question, for example, how my progress in that Japanese Zen practice was to be effectively monitored by teachers who did not speak Japanese and had never been to Japan – and whether I was even making any tangible progress at all by following their instructions.

What is more, these kinds of questions seemed to be taboo in most of the western Zen circles that I had experienced by that time – as well as any questioning of the asserted wisdom of senior practitioners. Rather, it seemed that one had to just place blind faith in such peoples' reported insights – their personal interpretations of the ancient teachings.

To me, this felt too dangerous – too great a risk, and especially so in light of the relatively recent scandals involving westerners who practiced 'blindly' within traditional Zen institutions.

And as if that were not enough – to top it all off,

when I sat in any of the traditional Japanese Zen meditation postures, my knees and ankles often felt, once again, like they were being damaged irreparably, and I was not able to relax as much as I wanted to.

I began suspecting, therefore, that something crucial was missing from these imported practices – something that I needed to discover for myself, perhaps some kind of yoga, lifestyle, or practical art element that was most likely located in a Zen art school or temple in the Far East.

I was hoping that I would be able to find that missing element, or set of elements, without having to spend years of my life travelling the planet, however – so that I could work and live comfortably and happily enough near my family and friends. And yet, eventually, after so much fruitless searching, one book, titled *Road to Heaven: Encounters with Chinese Hermits*, by Bill Porter, stirred up such a spirit of adventure within me – a burning desire to travel to the other end of the globe, all the way to China – the birthplace of Zen.

I thus handed in my resignation notice to my boss, obtained an English teaching qualification, bought a one-way ticket to China, and began to learn traditional Chinese arts in China not long after that.

Such a step required enduring a significant reduction in my monthly earnings, of course. And yet, I constantly encouraged myself to keep moving forwards – by recalling the words written to me by a good friend before he himself had left on a life-changing Zen quest – the phrase 'follow your heart.'

That was some time ago, and I am still in China

now – still following my heart as much as I can.

Nevertheless, over the years I have almost left this awesome country on a number of occasions. For by assuming that the remains of medieval China's golden age of Zen would still be accessible enough wherever I had decided to live and work, I had been sorely mistaken.

For example, in the Chinese city where I first arrived, I only managed to learn some basics of standing qigong meditation and a few principles of traditional Chinese landscape painting. And not long after that, upon finding myself in Beijing – China's state capital as well as cultural epicentre, I had only further succeeded in studying a little traditional Chinese DíZi flute, a few tai chi sword patterns, and some basic kung fu stretching.

In other words, I had still not found any practical arts that had actively encouraged or demanded any personal cultivation that was as remotely as deep as the meditation practice that I had learned from the Japanese Zen school in my British hometown.

By the time I arrived in Beijing, therefore, having travelled quite extensively in China – up, over, and through the most famous mountains and temples, I had actually become disillusioned as to the possibility of finding any existing non-monastic Zen masters or gifted layman teachers here. For Mao's Cultural Revolution had apparently been quite thorough in erasing the old ways and introducing the new ones.

For example, I had been told by well-educated Chinese people on a number of occasions that if I wanted to find the old Zen culture of China, I would need to go to Japan. This is because Chinese Zen had been particularly appreciated by the Japanese, who remain quite a conservative people even to this day.

So, in fact, I had arrived in Beijing as a stepping-stone – in order to upgrade my language teaching qualification, before heading to Japan. And yet, another episode of disappointment was to follow, as the Fukushima nuclear disaster occurred north of Tokyo, with its 'fallout' seeming to threaten to contaminate the area where I was intending to begin work.

Luckily, I had not bought my flight ticket to Tokyo, and my gut feeling was to allow it all to blow over somewhat – to tread water in Beijing and find an English teaching job here, before making any new radical decisions.

Looking back at that time, I now feel incredibly blessed that it was my fortune to meet such 'negative' conditions, though. For it was quite soon afterwards that I discovered in and around Beijing, tucked away out of sight – as one might expect with these kinds of humble activities, a number of authentic Zen arts alive and kicking in China.

They were, perhaps, only just surviving, or were keeping a low profile, but they were definitely vividly alive, nevertheless, and the doors of their schools were open to people like myself.

For example, I firstly discovered a Chinese zen calligraphy and tai chi teacher, called Paul Wang, and then his wife – a zen painting teacher, Jasmine Zhang. And shortly after this, I was quite randomly introduced to this planet's most developed international yiquan academy, which belongs to the legendary yiquan master Cuī Ruìbīn.

What is more, these teachers and their students also enjoyed practicing informal traditional Chinese zen tea rituals – the basics of which I began to pick up over numerous cups of green tea and tea-related discussions with them.

Thus, around eight years ago, I became immersed in a lifestyle that I had stopped believing was even possible to experience – a weekly schedule that, outside of my language teaching work, revolved around learning and enjoying traditional Chinese zen arts – disciplines that could be practiced as forms of meditation on a par with formal seated Zen meditation.

However, I will not pretend at this point that I was completely satisfied at that stage of my journey. For I was a little disappointed that all of my zen instructors, who are each extremely dedicated, talented, and apparently one of a kind in China, let alone the world, seemed to have their spiritual leanings angled firmly towards traditional Chinese Buddhism, even though none of them are ordained monks or nuns.

Such a situation was to be expected, I suppose, since Zen tends to be called Zen Buddhism, but I had also expected that there would have been less religious conviction driving their practices – and especially so in a Communism-oriented nation.

For even though I had my sympathies with their spiritual views, by that time I had begun to see Zen in a more modern scientific light. This was because, since the new millennium, western secular mindfulness (a form of meditation derived from Zen Buddhist practices) had been becoming increasingly mainstream.

This secularisation of Zen in the West had started decades before my adult life, in fact – in the seventies, after a MIT Ph.D. graduate, called Jon Kabat-Zinn, had conducted some pioneering scientific research into the healing potential of Buddhist meditation.

Kabat-Zinn's experiments revealed, for example, that a patient's recovery from the skin condition psoriasis occurred significantly faster when they had been guided in a form of traditional eastern seated Zen meditation – a practice that had been stripped of any mystical trappings so that it could be used in a modern western clinical setting.

After that methodological reframing, however, the technique employed during secular mindfulness meditation was still not much different from the formal seated Zen practice that Kabat-Zinn had learned from a traditional Korean Zen meditation teacher.

As a Zen saying goes, then, 'whatever works,' and so, after Kabat-Zinn's research was recognised by the scientific community, further studies were carried out in order to investigate the effects of mindfulness meditation on the brain, as well as on mood cycles and depressive behaviour.

These trials tended to revolve around administering a daily 'dose' of at least forty minutes of formal mindfulness meditation for a period of eight weeks, and resulted in the publication of further empirical insights into the powerful potential of mindfulness.

This was received very positively by the scientific community and media, and so a spirited western 'mindfulness revolution' began to gather significant momentum.

For example, in 2008, the Oxford Mindfulness Centre was set up within the Department of Psychiatry at the University of Oxford, which led to the publication of the book *Mindfulness: A Practical Guide to Finding Peace in a Frantic World*, written by Oxford university professor of clinical psychology Mark Williams, in collaboration with Danny Penman.

The book was a kind of supporting text for anyone taking part in what had come to be known as the standard eight week mindfulness-based stress reduction (MBSR) course (or its Cognitive Behavioural Therapy cousin – MBCT).

And although I was in China as all of this unfolded, I had been watching from abroad with great interest, because, in a way, the simple, direct, modern, scientifically- and clinically-vetted methodology particular to western secular mindfulness, as well as, to some extent, Japanese Sōtō Zen, was the kind of approach that I had travelled eastward in search of – albeit embedded within a practical art of some sort.

Now, however, what I had been seeking was being more thoroughly celebrated and explored where my journey had begun – within the practical arts of western clinical psychiatry and medicine.

What is more, as time went on, what had been labelled as a mere fad by some prominent early critics showed no sign of disappearing – perhaps because western scientific studies that rigorously researched the potential of mindfulness meditation continued, year on year, to reveal fresh positive findings – some of which were jaw-dropping.

For example, depressive relapses experienced by people with clinical depression were halved after the introduction of mindfulness meditation as an alternative treatment, and older people who practiced mindfulness meditation experienced a greater increase in the grey matter in their brains than their younger counterparts.

Thus, the growing popularity and effective use of this groundbreaking modern western scientific 'zen practice' was hailed as a revolution of sorts, and it was indeed a personal revolution for myself also. For as I read into the methodology and tested it personally by putting a daily secular mindfulness meditation practice in place, I began to notice how all areas of my life gradually became easier.

This insight in turn gave me extra momentum to harvest any wisdom from my zen teachers here in Beijing. And so, during my work week, I travelled from one zen art class to another, whilst simultaneously studying secular mindfulness at home.

But that was not all, for during the first three years of that period, I also spent every holiday living at Master Cui's International Yiquan Academy – in the countryside north of the capital, where I would train yiquan for six hours per day.

And I also continued to do yiquan posture work at home for at least one hour daily between such holidays, whilst also practicing seated meditation every morning for forty-five minutes as a kind of foundational meditation practice – a 'portable laboratory,' within which I would test out different practical approaches and ideas that I had collected from mindfulness books, videos, audio recordings, and my zen arts teachers' instructions.

Initially, I was very disappointed, since it seemed that western secular mindfulness clashed with much of the traditional Chinese Zen teachings. And yet, over time, as I continued to study and explore both the ancient Chinese and modern western 'Ways' first-hand, I found core overlaps that enabled me to use each individual art to support the other, and a kind of cross-pollination process began to occur.

I thus eventually discovered that these arts are, at their heart, all the same exercise – they can all be secular, scientifically-oriented formal mindfulness meditation practices, no matter their country or culture of origin.

A KEY: YIQUAN ZEN KUNGFU

A significant factor that helped me to gain the above insights was, as it happens, my choice to return to yiquan standing kung fu meditation. But it was not so much the standing still aspect as the explosive push-hands testing that really surprised and 'enlightened' me.

This is because yiquan push-hands tests one's momentary condition of body and mind – one's *true* progress in zen and mindfulness, through pretty rough combative exercises (movements that can translate directly into medieval hand-to-hand weapon thrusting and parrying) in such a way that *there can be no cheating* – no bending of the raw practical truth.

For with yiquan push-hands (or its extension into weapons sparring) the proof is very tangibly in the eating of the pudding, so to speak – one pushes or 'runs through' one's training partner, or one is pushed or 'run through' oneself.

And such competence is rarely something a person has been born with – it is never some innate animalistic reflex. Rather, it can only ever have been cultivated through diligent, disciplined, civil daily effort – through a noble kung fu regimen, that expands a person's mind and body towards ever-increasing potency.

Zen kung fu must therefore always involve a harnessing of the noble, civil potential that is possessed by every socialised human being. For the more peaceful and elegantly robust one is, then the more fluid and structurally sound one is, and the skillful manipulation of this sophisticated condition can enable one to remain relatively invulnerable to one's opponent's attacks.

On a very simple level, this seemingly mystical phenomenon can be explained away by the fact that uncivilised 'passive surrendering' to fear and mania ('passion') causes one to contract one's whole being, whilst a proactively civil – upright – gentlemanly peaceful heart, allows one to relax and expand one's being – so that one has more flexibility and potency, and thus a more grounded, internally calm condition.

Such physical and mental 'posturing' naturally gives

a pugilist of any sort more reach, fluidity, spontaneity in movement, and so on.

And so, in this particular respect, Zen kung fu is, in fact, no more potent or sophisticated than the western "gentlemanly" arts of boxing or fencing – disciplines that once promoted the martial benefits of civil values as expounded above (that is, before the widespread use of guns made traditional martial arts relatively redundant). And yet, the vision and potential heights of martial arts mastery, and the way for any relatively healthy person (not just the especially intuitive, physically robust, and naturally talented among us) to achieve that mastery, is a lot clearer when adhering to the traditional eastern approach to martial arts.

When talented western boxers pay a visit to Master Cui's yiquan school, therefore, they recognise how *all* the experienced yiquan boxers training there possess and utilise the very same 'power lines' that connect a gifted western boxer's feet to his hands – a whole body structural cohesion, that can generate considerable explosive power.

In the case of western-trained boxers, however, such mysterious, *seemingly super-human* power – the ability to knock out any opponent early on in a boxing bout, for example, often arises as a result of relatively random insights and intuition, as well as physiological 'innate gifts' honed when using the heavy bag and so forth – rather than as a result of any prolonged formal posture or stance coaching particular to the art of western boxing.

As far as yiquan is concerned, though, since it is not primarily sport-oriented, the most resilient and potent posture – one's general 'existential stance,' is the primary focus – a dynamic 'always on' expansion of mind and body, which is to be carried into the ever-changing, practical, *real* world – where inevitable adversity lurks, and referees or any formal 'rules to the game' are lacking.

However, this is not to say that yiquan boxers do not ever pressure test their art within a sportive martial arts context – far from it.

Master Cui's school has a Sǎndǎ (Chinese native MMA) section, for example, which regularly enters yiquan-trained kickboxers into competitions. And those fighters have tended to perform with considerable success. In fact, during my intensive training years at Master Cui's yiquan school, the main Sǎndǎ coach there – one of Cui's senior disciples, was a former China Sǎndǎ national champion.

Still, a sport requires rules – it is never a good enough model of the real world, and therefore does not allow for sufficient real world testing of a martial art.

Thus, the main emphasis within a yiquan training school tends to be, as already stated, the practitioner's 'always on' existential potency – their lifelong robust condition of body and mind, which includes the integrity of their path to mastery – whether they have the sufficient insight and wise support to maintain and develop their skill into later years (something which is undermined if a practitioner endures heavy blows to their head on a regular basis, of course).

This means that the ability to generate powerful energy from the soles of the feet upwards – akin to a gifted and intuitive western boxer, is seen as more of a side-effect of yiquan practice, rather than its core trait.

No matter such assertions having been relayed to me by European boxers who were training at master Cui's school, however, I was highly skeptical, at first, of the seemingly 'mystical' abilities that the art of yiquan was alleged to deliver to practitioners.

Eventually, though, after three years of solid daily yiquan practice, I could not deny the changes that had appeared within my own body – how my frame had opened up, for example, and how the new relationships and connections that had gradually manifested over the years as a result of that expansion could accomplish something new and seemingly 'super-human' when my posture was put under considerable pressure during push-hands testing.

Thus, as a result of persevering in enduring daily 'standing post' exercises, as well as the art of tussling with my fellow students at the yiquan school, I felt that a small miracle had occurred within the very fabric of my being.

And one of the most profound aspects was, for me, that it had occurred beyond the realm of words – from beyond any prescribed belief in the magical abilities of ancient kung fu wizards.

For it felt very real and 'normal,' in fact, and yet it was also quite empowering and encouraging. And the standing posture knee pain which had beleaguered me so much on previous occasions eventually disappeared, even – it had somehow been cured by the 'kung fu yoga.'

Introduction

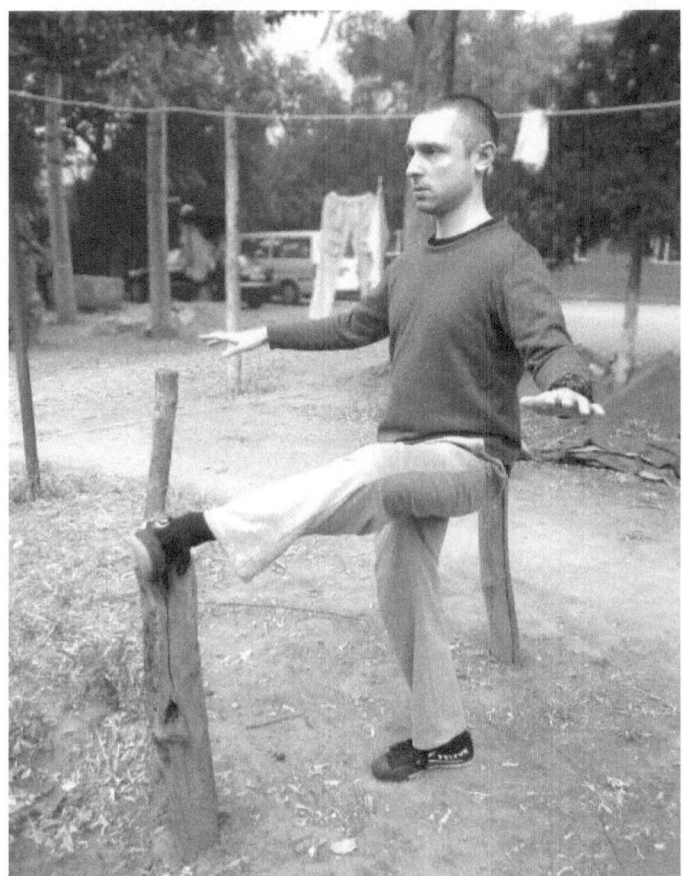

The author practicing a yiquan 'standing post' exercise at Master Cui's International Yiquan Academy, north of Beijing, in 2013.

A 'MISSION'

I began to feel rather fortunate in having experienced my fairly random encounters with zen arts masters. However, I also felt quite alone in my empowerment, for there was no one else that I could find online, let alone in China, who was studying these arts in the same way that I had been, and there still is not, as far as I am aware.

There arose within me, therefore, an impulse to share my knowledge with other people. And yet, I wanted to communicate the profundity of these various traditional Chinese zen disciplines from a more modern scientific perspective – so that they could be understood to overlap with the methodology of western secular mindfulness in the way that I myself had discovered them to – beyond the abstract subtleties of any mystical myths or hearsay.

I therefore completed an eight week MBSR course, and then attended a reputable western secular mindfulness instructor program in the U.K.

During that period, I studied, along with various NHS-employed clinical psychologists and physiotherapists, how to facilitate the standard eight week western secular mindfulness (MBCT) course meditations. And upon completion and receipt of my certification, I returned to China, where I have been hosting weekly secular mindfulness meditation and zen arts activities here in Beijing.

Right at this moment, then, I find myself to be the only person on our planet who has been instructing authentic western secular mindfulness classes in the context of having received, over a period of more than five years, weekly instruction from genuine Chinese lineage-holders in traditional Chinese zen calligraphy, zen painting, and zen kung fu – all at the same time.

It is my pleasure, therefore, and to an extent my responsibility, I feel, to share the profound methodological overlaps and elegant beauty of these

Introduction

arts with the world in a way that spans East and West, from ancient times to the present, and hopefully the distant future beyond.

Before we can embark together on such a journey, though, I will firstly need to provide a clearer picture of how western secular mindfulness and traditional Chinese Zen overlap methodologically – in a historical, as well as practical philosophical context that goes back in time thousands of years – to the beginning of Chinese history, even.

For once this developmental and practical environment has been made clear – in the simplest and briefest way available, then a penetration of traditional Chinese arts methodology can be obtained more effectively – via three Chapters dedicated to the disciplines of traditional Chinese Zen kung fu, Zen calligraphy, Zen ink painting, and Zen tea, respectively.

These exposés will then be followed by an epilogue that will bring all of the preceding Chapters together – through an illustration of how the various traditional Chinese Zen arts may be combined in order to create one big Zen path. For such an idea was prominent within Chinese society one thousand years ago, even – and apparently as far back as the time of Confucius, around 500 B.C.

So with this journey now laid out more clearly in front of us, let us move on to the next Chapter in order to better comprehend the overlaps between mindfulness and Zen – starting at the most logical place to achieve such an endeavor – at the very beginning of Chinese history.

I

MINDFULNESS AND ZEN

In a play called *Huis Clos*, by Sartre, the famously poignant line, "Hell is other people," is spoken.

It compels us to ask whether it is possible to more intelligently navigate all the inevitable changes of the human heart – all of our fickle loyalties and beliefs.

This question has been pursued by philosophers and mystics all over our planet since the dawn of history, it seems. And yet, as the Enlightenment philosopher David Hume pointed out, when we search for universal cyclical patterns of behaviour within our selves, all we find is constant change – a relentless flux.

We can assemble simplified, highly limited

predictive models of our fluid human condition, of course – involving the idea, for example, that people pass through summers and winters of the heart – with the cold-hearted often tending towards shameless parasitism, and the warm-hearted tending towards altruistic cooperation. It is just that when we try to monitor or manage this condition for prolonged periods of time, *it becomes an impossibly complex task.*

Perhaps this is because we humans have benefitted from developing increasingly complex interactions – giving rise to an increasingly complex sense of self, the subtleties of which we cannot discern – thus causing us to suffer a self-created 'imprisonment' within our mental forms.

If this is true, then as our societies have developed, maybe our lives have begun to feel increasingly empty of tangible meaning – of purpose, and direction.

However, in amongst this 'emptiness of self,' various observers have, at times, identified certain changes that they felt *were* repeated – dynamics that they deemed universal to all human hearts – with the ancient Chinese mystics in particular stating that these universal changes originate directly from the ever-transforming natural environment.

We know this because they recorded their findings for posterity – in the ancient Chinese book called the *Yìjīng* (易经), or *I-Ching – The Classic of Changes*, which dates back to before the eighth century B.C.

No matter its age, though, the *I-Ching* continues to remain quite prominent in the world today – not only in China, but also in the West – most often as a divination tool that provides comprehensive advice by way of a number of commentaries that were added to it from one century to the next.

In its most primitive form, however, it seems that the *I-Ching* was a collection of rather meagre, relatively abstract sentences that revolved around descriptions of natural phases – profound existential transition points, or nodes, that numbered sixty-four in total.

And yet, there was an additional highly mysterious dimension to this system, which involved the sequencing of its profound changes, or 'dynamic pictures.' For to each sentence was allocated a hexagram (six lines piled one above the other) that represented its number in binary form, and the overall sequence of these numbers was not particularly logical – most of them were arranged in a seemingly arbitrary fashion.

For example, the first hexagram in the sequence represents the binary number sixty-three, consisting of six unbroken lines – 'full yang,' and has the following most ancient 'advice' allocated to it:

乾:
Qián:
heavenly nature:

元	亨	利	贞
Yuán	Hēng	Lì	Zhēn
original	prosperity	benefitting	the virtuous

During the fifth century B.C., however, this sentence was apparently fleshed out, along with the other sixty-three statements that followed after it, by

Confucius, or perhaps a Confucian scholar who succeeded him, in order to create the more verbose standard advice that we find today.

The above first change (Qián), now begins as follows, therefore:

> *"Vast indeed is heavenly nature's origin, conceiving all things, and thereupon defining the heavens' details. Clouds transform into rain, objects are distributed into various forms. Greatly apparent in beginning and ending…"*

大	哉	乾	元,
Dà	Zāi	Qián	Yuán,
great	indeed	heavenly nature	originating

萬	物	资	始,
Wàn	Wù	Zī	Shǐ,
myriad	objects	of utility	conceived

乃	統	天.
Nǎi	Tǒng	Tiān.
then	interconnecting	the heavens

雲	行	雨	施,
Yún,	Xíng	Yǔ	Shī,
clouds	conduct	rains	executing

品	物	流	形.
Pǐn	Wù	Liú	Xíng.
classified	substances	spread	forms

大	明	始	終,
Dà	Míng	Shǐ	Zhōng,
greatly	apparent	(in) beginning	(and) ending

Such a description of the birth of a universe seems to have emerged from an inquiry into the true nature of our creative hearts – a cognitive process, which defines and labels details to the point that *we describe our own socially reflective selves into existence.*

This view on self-creation 'from nothingness' is not a rare insight, though, since even modern western mindfulness meditation practitioners are familiar with the process of impersonal 'cognitive emergence' – most likely as a result of their intimate encounters with their minds' often relentless internal dialogues.

Furthermore, it appears that Confucius was not the first ancient Chinese person to appreciate such a dimension to our condition. For the great sage did not claim his insights as his own. Instead, his exceptional practice was to engage in what he called 'recalling the ancient to know the modern' (WēnGùZhīXīn – 温故知新).

In other words, Confucius sourced much of his insight from ancient Chinese culture as it had been handed down to him from centuries before – via texts, rituals, music, and so on.

Whether the original insights behind the earliest *I-Ching* sentences were the same as those available to the Confucians who were embellishing them is not known, however, and perhaps never will be.

That being so, it seems that Confucius did take on

board much of the practical philosophy inspired by the *I-Ching*'s cosmological or broader cultural outlook – something which no doubt influenced many of the statements that he made during his lifetime, such as the following sentence in *The Analects* (*LúnYǔ* – 論語), Chapter 7 (Shù Ér – 述而), Verse 23:

> "The heavens granted me my virtue upon my creation."

天	生	德	於	予
Tiān	Shēng	Dé	Yú	Yǔ
the heavens	birthed	virtue	within	me

Confucius' proclamations regarding the absolute truth of his human condition did not go much further than this, however, since, as is stated in Chapter 5 (GōngYěCháng – 公冶长), Verse 13, the world of spoken doctrines is no place to find such insight:

> "...lectures about nature and the Way of the heavens cannot deliver the actual truth to listeners."

言	性	与	天	道
Yán	Xìng	Yǔ	Tiān	Dào
vocalising	the nature	allied with	the heavens'	Way

不	可	得	而	闻	也
Bù	Kě	Dé	Ér	Wén	Yě
not	possible	to obtain	whilst	hearing	it is so

And this sentiment is further confirmed in Chapter 17 (YángHuò – 陽貨), Verse 19 – where Confucius is asked by his disciples to provide them with teachings that they could record for posterity, to which he replies:

> *"Please allow me not to speak. [...] How do the heavens speak? The four seasons go about their business, and a great variety of objects are produced, so how do the heavens speak?!"*

予	欲	無	言	[...]
Yú	Yù	Wú	Yán	[...]
I	desire	non-	speaking	[...]

天	何	言	哉
Tiān	Hé	Yán	Zāi
the heavens	how	speak	alas?

四	時	行	焉
Sì	Shí	Xíng	Yān
four	seasons	conduct	herein

百	物	生	焉
Bǎi	Wù	Shēng	Yān
hundred	substances	birthed	herein

天	何	言	哉
Tiān	Hé	Yán	Zāi?
the heavens	how	speak	alas?!

And yet, no matter his making such statements, people continued to latch onto and worship

Confucius' words – memorising them as if they were a magical formula or spell that would somehow, by mere repetition alone, deliver the virtuous path – the Way, or 'Dào' (in Chinese), that their master spoke of.

This was even after Confucius had directly referred to such rote learning behavior as being ineffectual – in *The Analects* (Chapter 13 (ZǐLù – 子路), Verse 5):

"Three hundred Odes memorised,
given powers to govern,
but not accomplished well.

When dispatched to the four quarters,
not competent in special relations.

Though many Odes are learned, why
ending up acting in this way?"

诵	诗	三	百
Sòng	Shī	Sān	Bǎi
reciting	odes	three	hundred

授	之	以	政
Shòu	Zhī	Yǐ	Zhèng
investiture	held	in order to	govern

不	达
Bù	Dá
not	accomplished

使	于	四	方
Shǐ	Yú	Sì	Fāng
dispatched	to	the four	quarters

Mindfulness and Zen

不	能	专	对
Bù	Néng	Zhuān	Duì
not	competent in	special	relations

虽	多
Suī	Duō
though	well-provided

亦	奚	以	为
Yì	Xī	Yǐ	Wéi
yet	why	accordingly	acting?

However, the Confucians continued to persist in their rote learning.

Perhaps it was mostly because, by the time of the Han Dynasty, government office entrance exams – written tests that required candidates to have mastered Confucius' recorded teachings, had been introduced.

That being so, maybe some scholars who rote learned Confucian texts would also seek to 'get in the groove' of, and thus inherit, the wisdom – the 'mind stream,' of Confucius' particular Way, akin to Buddhist monks who chanted the words of their enlightened master.

In fact, such attempts to access wisdom through the mastery of another's 'wise words,' or 'Way,' was explicitly addressed by another Chinese sage; namely, Confucius' most famous antagonist – the Daoist (or Taoist) master known as LaoTzu, in his book *DàoDéJīng* (or *Tao Teh Ching*).

However, LaoTzu's view on becoming attached to

words was seemingly not much different to Confucius'. For LaoTzu states at the very beginning of the *DàoDéJīng* (Chaper 1):

> "A way that is called The Way is not the absolute Way. A name that is called The Name is not an absolute name.
>
> The nameless represents the beginning of the heavens and earth, while the named is the mother of all myriad objects.
>
> Thus, transcend desires in order to observe such subtleties, and indulge desires in order to know limitations."

道	可	道	非	常	道
Dào	Kě	Dào	Fēi	Cháng	Dào
way	favoured	way	not	always	The Way

名	可	名	非	常	名
Míng	Kě	Míng	Fēi	Cháng	Míng
name	favoured	name	not	always	The Name

無	名
Wú	Míng
(when) not	naming

Mindfulness and Zen

天	地	之	始
Tiān	Dì	Zhī	Shǐ
the heavens	(and) earth	have	a beginning

有	名
Yǒu	Míng
(when) having	a name

萬	物	之	母
Wàn	Wù	Zhī	Mǔ
myriad	objects	have a	mother

故	常	無	欲
Gù	Cháng	Wú	Yù
thus	always	(when) not	desiring

以	觀	其	妙
Yǐ	Guān	Qí	Miào
so	observe	their	subtlety

常	有	欲
Cháng	Yǒu	Yù
(when) always	having	desire

以	觀	其	徼
Yǐ	Guān	Qí	Jiǎo
so	observe	their	limits

Here, LaoTzu seems to be inferring that if we want to know who or what we *truly* are – our true heart or mind that governs each of our behaviours, we must first truly know the cosmos – the heavens and earth that give rise to our minds and bodies in the first place. And this necessarily requires a discernment of nature's subtleties beyond the relatively murky concept-driven ways of being – beyond words, semantics, cultural bias, and so on. For LaoTzu clearly states, 'when not naming, the heavens and earth have a beginning.'

He also infers that in order to successfully go beyond the naming – to observe these 'subtle beginnings' of the true heavens and earth that created us, and thus the true nature that governs our hearts, we have to master our often insatiable appetites for "naming and claiming" – our attachment to seductive labels and symbols, that can so easily rule our lives.

For instead, we just need to *be* – a sentiment that even western philosophers such as Heidegger took to heart. Because in that experience of pure being, we may detect a certain signature particular to the physical truth – *an existential flow* uniting all of nature, and thus the *dynamic essence* of the 'big bang,' the cosmos, or whatever other mere label one prefers.

And yet, just like Confucius, LaoTzu could of course downplay the potential of words all he liked, whilst it was pretty obvious to all people receiving his teachings – *via his words* – that the economic benefits of being able to use such symbols were considerable.

For words significantly empower us in a potentially infinite number of ways – just like mathematical quantities and formulae do, and so it is very easy to expect that such concept-driven calculating can solve all of our problems.

Thus, the majority of ancient Chinese people apparently continued to search for spoken answers to their predicaments no matter Confucius' and LaoTzu's recommendations.

But what words can truly communicate colour to someone who has been born blind? Or the feeling of falling in love to someone who has never experienced that condition before? So there was, and still is, a natural physical world out there – a purely practical world *existing beyond concepts and words*, that ultimately 'calls the shots.'

It is just that it seems it takes some time for a society to be 'ready' to move on and fully embrace that ultimate 'unnamable truth,' or 'spirit' of nature, wholeheartedly. Thus, it appears that China was just not ready enough for such a broad shift in cultural outlook during the time of Confucius and LaoTzu.

Around one thousand years later, however, things had changed, and were about to change even more, due to the arrival in China of the first patriarch of Zen – a man called Bodhidharma (DáMó – 达摩), who was an Indian, or perhaps Persian, master of Buddhist dhyana (Zen – Chán (禅)) meditation.

For upon Bodhidharma's discovering that Chinese Buddhist monks were taking the metaphors in their scriptures literally, and thus practicing Buddhism incorrectly, he decided to rectify their approach by allegedly teaching the following:

> *"External instructions do not transmit effectively,*
>
> *So therefore do not elevate scriptural doctrines.*
>
> *Just point directly to the human heart,*

In order to be true Buddha Nature in motion."

達	磨	四	聖	句
Dá	Mó	Sì	Shèng	Jù
Bodhidharma		Four	Sacred	Sentences

教	外	別	傳
Jiào	Wài	Bié	Zhuàn
Instructing	external	does not	transmit.

不	立	文	字
Bù	Lì	Wén	Zì
Do not	elevate	scriptural	words.

直	指	人	心
Zhí	Zhǐ	Rén	Xīn
Directly	point to	human	heart/mind.

見	性	成	佛
Jiàn	Xìng	Chéng	Fó
Demonstrate	character	developing	Buddha.

Bodhidharma's message here seems clear enough – that words must be transcended if one wishes to make contact with the ultimate truth of our human condition.

And so, in this way, the first patriarch of Zen's stance appears congruent with LaoTzu and Confucius' teachings regarding naming objects – specifically the importance of stopping living through the manipulation of concepts – mental imagery, and to instead witness the direct truth of one's nature – one's "heavenly-bestowed" virtuous heart, *first-hand*.

Mindfulness and Zen

And such a position was to be further echoed in a later Zen text, called *Faith in Mind Inscription* (*XìnXīn Míng* – 信心銘) – a treatise often thought to have been composed in sixth century China by the third patriarch of Zen, which begins as follows:

> *"Arriving at The Way is not difficult, simply stop announcing preferences.*
>
> *Only do not love or hate in order to understand things clearly.*
>
> *A thousandth of a hair's discrepancy, and the heavens and the earth dangle separated.*
>
> *In desiring to grasp the truth of the present moment, do not attach to what is favoured or unfavoured."*

至	道	无	难,			
Zhì	Dào	Wú	Nán,			
Arriving	the Way	not	difficult,			

				唯	嫌	拣	择.
				Wéi	Xián	Jiǎn	Zé.
				simply	shun	adopting	preferences.

但	莫	憎	爱,
Dàn	Mò	Zēng	Ài,
Only	must not	hate	and love,

洞	然	明	白.
Dòng	Rán	Míng	Bái.
fathom	and then	know	clearly.

毫	厘	有	差,
Háo	Lí	Yǒu	Chā,
Hair	thousandth	has	discrepancy,

天	地	悬	隔.
Tiān	Dì	Xuán	Gé.
the heavens	and earth	dangle	separated.

欲	得	现	前,
Yù	Dé	Xiàn	Qián,
Desiring	to grasp	what is manifesting	before one,

莫	存	顺	逆.
Mò	Cún	Shùn	Nì.
must not	cherish	adhering	(and) denouncing.

Again, we see in the above words a reference to the original oneness of the heavens and earth being lost when a person creates discrepancies between things – as the result of a judging mind that seeks conceptual, verbal answers to everything.

And this is a very practical insight to recognise, for the ultimate answers to our mundane daily problems – such as dirty dishes, tiredness, or feeling thirsty, are never verbal. Instead, their ultimate solutions arise *through pure action*.

In fact, this sentiment is not even limited to Bodhidharma's Zen – it is present in the Buddha's original words. For example, in the *Vimalakīrti Sūtra* and the *Laṅkāvatāra Sūtra*, the Buddha explains that all concepts are illusions, and are therefore not to be attached to, because language does not represent the truth of the practical reality in which we live.

So Chinese Zen Buddhism in particular teaches a practical philosophy that is in harmony with Confucianism and Daoism – in the sense that it aims towards a path, a *Dao*, that is beyond mere philosophy – *beyond words*.

It aims, rather, towards the domain of physical cycles and subconscious natural intent inherited from the earth, the heavens, and their chemical elements.

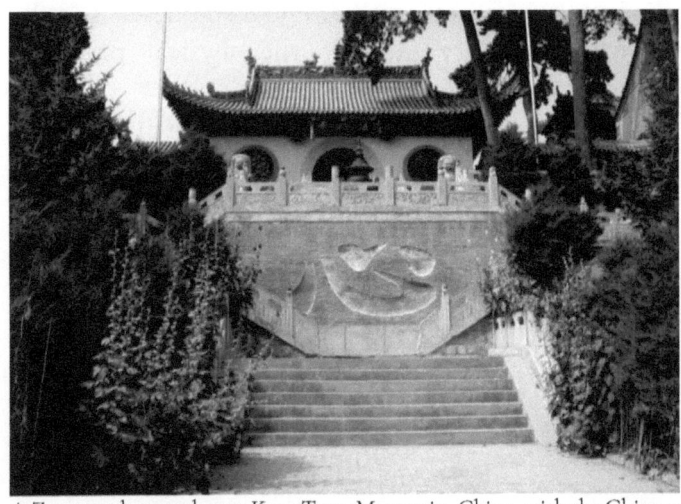

A Zen temple complex on KongTong Mountain, China, with the Chinese character for heart/mind (Xīn – 心) carved into the wall at the entrance.

And western secular mindfulness' aim is no different in this respect – perhaps unsurprisingly so, even, because, as mentioned in the previous chapter, it inherited its core approach from Zen Buddhist teachers – meditation masters, who in turn inherited their essential methodology from Bodhidharma.

As a result of this inheritance, one often finds within secular mindfulness an emphasis on pursuing the 'being mode,' rather than the 'doing mode,' for example.

For setting the aim to flow in harmony with the direct nature of the present moment (being) is directly opposed to taking one's behavioural cues from any random assumptions arriving in one's awareness (doing), since grasping at such anthropocentric fabrications – shallow symbols, is literally 'living a lie' – it instantly creates conflict between oneself and the ultimate 'authority'; namely, the physical, practical, indisputable laws of nature.

Thus, the 'being mode' has been, and still is, highly valued in formal Chinese Zen doctrine, and is referred to as WúWéi (无为) – literally, 'non-enacting.'

In fact, WúWéi was originally mentioned by Confucius in *The Analects*, Chapter 15 (WèiLíngGōng – 卫灵公), Verse 5, as follows:

"Non-enacting to govern,
King Shun followed it indeed.

How is it enacted?!

One's self politely and uprightly facing
the heavenly sunshine, and then
stopping!"

无	为	治	者
Wú	Wéi	Zhì	Zhě
non-	enacting	to govern	;

其	舜	也	与
Qí	Shùn	Yě	Yǔ
that	King Shun	was so	with it

夫	何	为	哉
Fū	Hé	Wéi	Zāi
this	how	enacted	?!

恭	己	正	南	面
Gōng	Jǐ	Zhèng	Nán	Miàn
politely	one's self	uprightly	South	-facing

而	已	矣
Ér	Yǐ	Yǐ
and then	stopping	!

However, the Daoist sage LaoTzu tends to be thought of as the main proponent of ancient Chinese WúWéi. For example, in *DàoDéJīng*, Chapter 2, he states:

> *"Wise humans administrate their business by non-enacting, going forth without formalising their doctrine."*

圣	人	处
Shèng	Rén	Chù
wise	humans	administrate

无	为	之	事
Wú	Wéi	Zhī	Shì
non-	enacting	their	matters

行	不	言	之	教
Xíng	Bù	Yán	Zhī	Jiào
going forth	not	vocalising	their	doctrine

And in Chapter 43:

"The most adaptable of the heavens' subordinates swiftly gallops beyond the most rigid of the heavens' subordinates.

Not holding on, one enters into no dominion, and thus accordingly knows the benefits of non-enacting.

Its doctrine indescribable, the benefits of non-enacting are rarely attained by the heavens' subordinates."

天	下	之	至	柔
Tiān	Xià	Zhī	Zhì	Róu
the heavens'	Inferiors'	own	most	adaptable

驰	骋
Chí	Chěng
swiftly	gallops beyond

Mindfulness and Zen

天	下	之	至	坚
Tiān	Xià	Zhī	Zhì	Jiān
the heavens'	Inferiors'	own	most	firm

无	有	入	无	间
Wú	Yǒu	Rù	Wú	Jiàn
non-	holding	going into	non-	dominion

吾	是	以	知
Wú	Shì	Yǐ	Zhī
one	thus	accordingly	knowing

无	为	之	有	益
Wú	Wéi	Zhī	Yǒu	Yì
non-	enacting's	own	held	benefits

不	言	之	教
Bù	Yán	Zhī	Jiào
not	vocalising	its	doctrine

无	为	之	益
Wú	Wéi	Zhī	Yì
non-	enacting's	own	benefits

天	下	希	及	之
Tiān	Xià	Xī	Jí	Zhī
the heavens'	inferiors	rarely	reaching	it

And this emphasis on existing without adhering to any doctrine – *just being what one is*, explicitly framed as existing in humble harmony with the practical 'superior' law, or Way, of the heavens, is another theme common to both Confucius and LaoTzu, in fact.

For in *The Confucian Book of Rites* (*Lǐjì* – 禮記), for

example – in Chapter 31 (ZhōngYōng – 中庸), which is a famous text known as *The Doctrine of the Mean*, the Confucians state (Verse 22):

"Generating sincerity is the heavens' inherent Way.

Generating the sincere-oriented is humans' inherent Way.

Generating sincerity requires not endeavouring, and so centredness remains.

Not conceiving, and so fully grasping.

Following along with ease, and centred when in among ways, are the wiser humans."

诚	者
Chéng	Zhě
making sincere	;

天	之	道	也
Tiān	Zhī	Dào	Yě
the heavens'	inherent	Way	it is so

诚	之	者
Chéng	Zhī	Zhě
making sincere	-oriented	;

人	之	道	也
Rén	Zhī	Dào	Yě
Humans'	inherent	Way	it is so

诚	者
Chéng	Zhě
making sincere	;

不	勉	而	中
Bù	Miǎn	Ér	Zhōng
not	endeavouring	and so	centred amidst

不	思	而	得
Bù	Sī	Ér	Dé
not	conceiving	and so	fully grasping

从	容	中	道
Cóng	Róng	Zhōng	Dào
following	with ease	(and) centred amidst	ways

圣	人	也
Shèng	Rén	Yě
wise	humans	it is so

In a similar vein, meanwhile, LaoTzu states, in Chapter 73 of *DàoDéJīng*:

> "The heavens' inherent Way never contends and so wins virtuously.
>
> It never formulates a doctrine and so responds virtuously.

It is never summonable and so it arrives independently.

It is unattached thus, and so strategises virtuously."

天	之	道
Tiān	Zhī	Dào
the heavens'	inherent	Way

不	争	而	善	胜
Bù	Zhēng	Ér	Shàn	Shèng
not	contending	and so	virtuously	winning

不	言	而	善	应
Bù	Yán	Ér	Shàn	Yīng
not	vocal	and so	virtuously	responding

不	召	而	自	来
Bù	Zhào	Ér	Zì	Lái
not	summonable	and so by	itself	coming hither

繟	然	而	善	谋
Chǎn	Rán	Ér	Shàn	Móu
unattached	thus	and so	virtuously	strategising

Such an emphasis on tuning oneself to the tangible laws of the heavens – of 'what is', and then seeking to exist intelligently – wisely, 'just being' – in harmony with those laws via 'non-doing,' was not even restricted to eastern philosophy in the ancient world, though.

For the ancient Greek philosopher Heraclitus, who was close to the founders of what we today call western science, made some very similar statements – albeit in rather meagre fragments, since they are the only teachings of his that have survived to the present day.

In the longest fragment of Heraclitus' original philosophy, for example, which is the beginning of a work called *On Nature*, he promotes his idea of a 'Logos' – a logical verbal account of nature's universal laws, which is a parallel concept, arguably, to the Dao or 'Way of the Heavens' of the ancient Chinese philosophers, as well as the Buddhists' Dhamma – teachings on the empirical truth of existence.

For Heraclitus' communicated Logos poetically attributes the arising of all objects to the perpetual changing of the seasons, with his idea of a wise life being to proactively speak and act in accordance with that cosmic natural truth as it arrives to one.

However, similarly to LaoTzu and Confucius' teachings, Heraclitus' fragments claim that his logical expounding on the nature of each phenomenon is most often incomprehensible to the average man, since the truth of nature 'loves to remain obscure' – hidden from view, in the same way that a human soul so often is.

Therefore, Heraclitus also asserted that the Logos belongs to our subtle divine essence – to the broader soul of man, which he framed as being eternal and infinite – ever-present – and fed by one divine natural law common to all people, so that we may all come to know that law as we follow the Logos, and be deeply nourished by its profound nature.

And even though Heraclitus stated that this knowledge could not be obtained by simply labelling and comparing all the various objects contained within our universal nature, he considered – perhaps in the same spirit as Confucius did, that such a path – such a *scholastic mode* of labelling and classifying natural objects as they arrived to one's senses (so that their details could be communicated to others), had delivered to him relatively unique and profound insights.

Thus, in the context of his eastern counterparts' assertions, Heraclitus' most radical belief was that a verbalised account of universal natural laws – a Logos, *should* be assembled. For although a Logos was often incomprehensible to the masses, it had its relevant place – its own particular value, in the human world.

And it seems that Confucius and LaoTzu would have agreed with Heraclitus on this point – that any sincerely expounded natural Way holds inherent usefulness or potency – *albeit in context*. Otherwise, why did these sages bother saying anything at all?

Verbal accounts of the absolute truth, therefore – of the experience of pure being, are not in themselves 'bad.' Indeed, it seems that the formalised construction of a Logos can be a profound 'Way,' even – a spiritual practice or ritual in its own right.

And as it happens, one of Heraclitus' such constructed accounts – his famous declaration that a river is never the same river, that it is always changing, impermanent – empty of anything more than its fluid nature, is often mentioned when scholars discuss ancient Greek philosophy in the context of Buddhism. For the 'law of impermanence' was, and still is, a famous Buddhist tenet around which all Buddhist teachings, the Dhamma, revolve.

And yet, if the Dhamma, or Heraclitus' Logos, are themselves run through with impermanence, then the absolute truth that such doctrines seek to represent must be infinitely changeable – in every moment and for every person. Thus, in the Buddhist text *Mahāparinibbāna Sutta*, for example, Gautama Buddha tells his disciple Ananda that when seeking refuge in Dhamma – in existential truth, then its tangible 'form' should be as a 'personal island' – *one's own uniquely experienced moment-to-moment Way*.

What is more, Gautama relates that this understanding can only be arrived at after 'earnestly' – sincerely, and therefore mindfully, comprehending the cosmos as it arrives at one's senses – by one letting go of *trying to be* some pre-formulated, rigid, limited idea of a natural human.

Instead, the Buddha makes it clear that all efforts should be put into becoming a human *just being – flowing naturally, and thus liberated from all self-created fetters*.

For Buddhists in particular, however, this can only occur after they have mastered the eight 'Right' practices of the Buddhist Noble Eightfold Path; namely, Right View, Right Resolve, Right Speech, Right Conduct, Right Livelihood, Right Effort, Right Mindfulness, and Right Concentration.

In being *practices*, though, they are not just philosophies to be contemplated for entertainment purposes – or as distant ideals, even. Rather, they are to be engaged with intimately – experienced first-hand, in order to be truly known and understood.

In this light, then, any talk of Dhamma, Dao, Logos,

or Zen Buddhism in general, that remains limited to the domain of mental gymnastics – to the mere comparison of famous teachers' words and historical actions, is what some respected Zen teachers have called "Zen bullshit."

And the same goes for any empty talk regarding secular mindfulness meditation. For even though Right Mindfulness is the seventh step on the traditional Buddhist Eightfold Path, as an anchoring skill (via Ānāpānasati breathing, for example) – a kind of mental preparation for the final eighth step of Right Concentration, western secular mindfulness incorporates what are often referred to as 'choiceless awareness' or 'spacious awareness' meditations into its approach, which are more advanced Right Concentration style practices.

Thus, secular mindfulness brings Buddhist Right Mindfulness practices together with Buddhist Right Concentration practices – creating one unified meditative continuum in the process.

In fact, this latter practice of Right Concentration is where the word zen came from in the first place, since zen, or 'Chán' (禅), is the Chinese pronunciation of the Pali word jhāna (in Sanskrit: 'dhyana'), which means 'absorption' – with 'jhana work' arguably being the main focus of Buddhist Right Concentration practice.

Therefore, secular mindfulness, as a formal approach, simply seeks to firstly establish the ability to focus on narrowed, yet deeply soothing, anchors for sustained periods of time (similarly to Right Mindfulness), and as the practitioner becomes more competent – as their sustained concentration ability improves, then broadened anchors are introduced.

In this way, the practitioner can eventually feel confident in 'just being with what is' – being able to concentrate on the broader perspective of existence 'choicelessly' and 'spaciously' for sustained periods of time (Right Concentration; 'jhana work'; zen).

And this compounding of the final two stages of the Buddhist Eightfold Path into one blended, yet still relatively graduated practice means that Buddhist Right Mindfulness practices are thus less potent, and less 'Zen,' than western secular mindfulness meditations in general. Therefore, as formal disciplines, mindfulness (which in this book means modern secular mindfulness) and Zen are mostly the same – especially when it comes to not consciously calculating and 'doing' (via spacious/choiceless awareness), and thus not applying prescribed formulas.

For they are, rather, things to *be* – *via a letting go of prescriptions*, a dropping of formalised doctrines in general, with the less being stated about that the better, perhaps, so that one can 'get into the groove' – *feel the flow, and follow along with that natural wholesome momentum*, in as direct a way as possible.

And yet, the differences between the two – the 'doing of the method' and the 'being of the method,' can be subtle, of course. And this is probably one contributing reason as to why there are so many resources published that intend to help with that issue.

For it is impossible to begin a practice of intending to 'let go' – in order to flow impersonally with the conditions of the present moment, without a self-critical perspective – something which inevitably prevents us from relaxing and flowing in any way whatsoever!

And so this is the biggest hurdle to overcome for both mindfulness and Zen practitioners – to let go of what we *think* should exist according to our engineered mental constructs – our judging mind, and just accept, as best we can, the laws of nature as they exist right here, right now – to directly witness any of our imperfections as perfect in the context of a functional cosmos.

Such a surrendering to our uglier, or perhaps organic, truths is easier said than done, however. Because it can often seem wiser to choose a conservative approach over a more congruous one – an immortality fantasy over our predictable death, for example – like wearing a youthful-looking guise over one that reveals our true age, procrastinating instead of chasing our dreams, or choosing to impose authority and supervise others – as if we are a deity of some sort, rather than work hard ourselves.

For it seems that most people make at least one of the above choices every day, even though it tends to give them 'complexes' – it literally complicates and dissociates their practical lives to the point that they become more dysfunctional.

Relative to all that complexity, however, the method of accepting our organic truth is rather simple. It merely requires shifting one's attention away from stressors and towards a source of wholesome peace that is present in one's immediate environment – an 'anchor.'

This anchor could be the harmonious social congruence felt when speaking productively with a good friend, appreciating soothing music, or flowing with the graceful movements of the body whilst dancing or painting.

It could also be found by simply tuning into the smooth, silk-like sensations of one's breath around and within one's nostrils, appreciating one's diaphragm reflexively massaging the belly from above, or even just fully occupying the space – the latent inherent peace, of the present moment itself with one's awareness.

It may thus be recognised that these attentional choices create so many opportunities for all aspects of a person's daily routine to become mindfulness meditation or 'zen' – a positive congruity with 'what is,' which can help one to accept the broader truth of one's natural existence – no matter whether one is cleaning, exercising, eating, writing, socialising with friends, and so on. It can all be experienced as impersonal flow – where one forgets the burden of one's selfish whims and time flies, as the wholesome fun just keeps on arriving.

That is the ideal, of course, which is very difficult to achieve for most of our waking hours, because our faith in good friends, our bodies, and in peaceful conditions themselves, can, due to life's ups and downs, be notably less than what we were born with.

Thus, the term 'practice' is used a lot in mindfulness and Zen – a practicing of 'being okay,' as best one can, with all the random yet potentially harrowing loss that is constantly occurring within and around one.

For the fact, in any case, that we were all born

screaming – that we were ejected from the effortless existence that we had been enjoying in our mother's wombs, into spine-chilling vulnerability, gives us enough propaganda for cynicism regarding the 'truth' of what a womb-like condition of peace seems to promise – namely, an extremely painful wake-up call after nine months of growing accustomed to it!

And yet, both mindfulness and Zen aim to transcend this 'propaganda of depression' – the idea that inner peace is just a sick joke – that its potential, say, to help us improve our work life, or our failing marriage, is a losers game. For this latter perception has, throughout human history all over the world, needed to be turned on its head via the application of practical philosophy – *the art of living more wisely*, if our societies were not to implode with mental illness and violence.

We may find, therefore, at certain key points in our lives, an appetite for 'turning things around.' And we can start this process by reframing any unavoidable sickness – any dis-ease and depression, generated by such asymmetries as the random distribution of wealth and marital satisfaction, as being just a necessary natural condition of the universe. For without such asymmetry there would not be any uniqueness – no particular strengths to be accumulated over a lifetime, nor any particular weaknesses, either.

In other words, without existential asymmetry there would be nothing that makes us special and uniquely 'us' as individuals.

When misfortune *must* arrive, then, it is not wise to actively resist it – by way of power struggles built around rigid belief systems, or any other kind of incongruous imposition. For if one does indulge in such disharmonious behaviour, one simply gives any chaotic forces additional energy.

Rather, the most practical solutions to maintaining an ordered life in amongst unavoidable asymmetries can only ever involve physical and mental acceptance – true inner peace, where one allows any imbalances to work themselves out in their own time – with misfortunes becoming blessings one moment, and blessings becoming misfortunes the next, and so on – as they have done over the thousands of years of human civil development.

At this point, however, one may be asking why traditional Chinese Zen had to be repackaged for a western audience in the form of secular mindfulness. For if the traditional Chinese teachings were so congruent with all human civil philosophies, could they not just be directly translated instead of there having to be this new secular mindfulness movement?

The answer to this question seems to be that by the time the West had opened itself up intellectually to traditional Chinese wisdom, China was already several hundred years forward from its own 'mindfulness revolution,' and had also suffered the Mongol invasions, which had changed the Chinese socio-political and spiritual landscape somewhat.

For the Mongols struck military deals with Tibetan Buddhist leaders so that they could extend their religious influence deeper into the rest of China, and by that time, the behaviours and words of traditional Zen masters had been studied so carefully, and for hundreds of years, that it was becoming difficult to distinguish between who had genuine insight, or who was merely a good actor parroting or re-wording the insights of others.

In this regard, then, it seems that China's Zen culture had grown into a tangled forest, within which it was easy to become lost or ensnared.

What was needed, perhaps, was a good forest fire to see which strands of Zen culture were truly the most practical, and therefore resilient.

And this tangled history would appear to explain, for example, why, during my many years living in China, not once has a Chinese person ever championed the patriarchs of Zen when the topic of Chinese Buddhism has been brought up. Their first response, rather, has been to recommend a visit to Tibet.

Hopefully such an anecdote can begin to illustrate, therefore, the complexity of Chinese Buddhism and its variety of schools and doctrines, and thus its various methodologies for arriving at buddhahood.

For the Chinese Zen tradition can itself be broken down into different schools that emphasise different practice methods – something which sets the scene for doctrinal conflict right from the outset, before one even arrives in Tibet.

In the hope of maintaining simplicity, then, this book is primarily concerned with the Zen methodology that is rooted in traditional teachings attributed to the early Chinese Zen patriarchs, as well as the ancient Chinese philosophical sages that those teachers drew metaphors and examples from before all of the above complexity was created.

In fact, it even seems that Zen arose in China as an attempt to *transcend the conflict that inevitably emerges from intellectual complexity – in order to consolidate and unify* the major competing philosophical traditions; namely, Daoism, Confucianism, and Buddhism, that were often causing sociopolitical turbulence from one dynasty or ruler to the next.

Thus, within Chen style tai chi, for example – a martial art that places the Daoist 'yin-yang' symbol on its banner, one finds a movement called 'Buddha's attendant pounds the mortar' (JīnGāngDǎoDuì – 金刚捣碓), which makes sense, because the martial art in fact originates from Shaolin Temple – the legendary birthplace of Chinese Zen Buddhism and Zen kung fu!

In this regard, original Shaolin Zen kung fu, as a root spiritual and health preserving practice for traditional Chinese Zen monks, served as a kind of practical anchor that cut through any doctrinal differences between Zen schools, and indeed traditional doctrines of any sort – just as mixed martial arts (MMA) competitions are doing in the world of traditional martial arts at present.

For 'trial by combat' operates within the purely physical domain, where the biological struggle to survive takes place – beyond labels and historical biases. Therefore, the outcome of a professional push-hands or MMA bout rests in *the application of fine skill whilst under duress*, and this is where mindfulness and Zen can really make a difference – as the samurai warriors of medieval Japan famously discovered.

Even in our modern age, though, the potential competitive advantage of a more mindful approach to overcoming physical adversity continues to be confirmed – by many successful Olympic athletes, for example, as well as tennis and basketball champions, who have attributed their highest achievements to the inclusion of western secular mindfulness meditation in their practice regimen.

And it seems that newcomers continue to get on board this 'success vehicle' in ever-increasing numbers. For if there is less busy-ness occupying and potentially obstructing one's mind, then one will be less likely to miss something important – a flaw in one's game plan, or a key obstacle to gaining a promotion, for example, since, as the saying goes, 'the devil is in the detail.'

The world is apparently rediscovering, then, that the most effective way to identify life's subtle yet significant pitfalls – the devilish finer details that cause us so much potentially unnecessary suffering, is to allow the swirling clouds of dust to settle – to bring more peace into one's heart, by easing it into harmony with the very nature that gives rise to and sustains it.

Thus, mindfulness and Zen are ultimately performance-enhancing practices that are supposed to make all aspects of one's existence more enjoyable and harmonious – to the point, even, whereby one may transcend one's 'birth trauma' and find eternal peace – so that one can flow along in perfect harmony with the laws and elements of nature – just like the ants, the birds, the flowers, trees, and the Sun and the Moon.

As a mindfulness saying goes, therefore, 'there is nothing to do, but there is plenty to *be*,' and mindfulness practices help us to 'get in the groove' in this regard.

In fact, these arts, no matter whether attributed to formal mindfulness or Zen, are just a means to an end – a raft to go from one shore to another – from an experience of general unease to a deeply harmonious flow. And such effortless and positive flow, which the ancient Greeks apparently referred to as *eudaimonia*, is so enjoyable when it occurs that one is too busy enjoying it to even reflect on how enjoyable it is!

We all know this state – having lost the sense of time whilst engaged in some wholesome activity, flowing with present conditions as they arrive and intermingle – perhaps whilst socialising, painting, relaxing on a beach, reading, and so on – as described in the acclaimed book *Finding Flow*, by Mihaly Csikszentmihalyi.

For during flow, we momentarily 'lose ourselves,' but it is not a tragic descent – it is not us becoming 'a nobody.' We are, instead, just too engaged – *too in harmony with the now*, to be concerned with ego-driven agendas, or the passage of time, even.

This is the true goal of both Zen and mindfulness – the mind filling the infinite space of the present moment.

As a direct experience, it is also the tangible manifestation of buddha, true nature, the Dao, Oneness, congruence, harmony, the divine, the spirit of the good life – the 'godly' life, or whatever other label one wishes to give it. The words do not really matter, because it is primarily *a pure feeling*, rather than an idea.

Such a condition of being even arrives to us, at times, without any formal effort having been needed beforehand. And as a result, Zen masters tend to laugh a lot about our human condition – as they realise that before they achieved enlightenment, no matter where they had gone, or to whom they had spoken, this eternal, infinite Oneness of non-self and non-temporality – this omnipresent positive potential or diamond-like 'jewel,' had been available all along – waiting there in their pockets for them to access and enjoy at any time. They had just been too busy *thinking* otherwise.

And so, the enlightened state *is* something real – *it is attainable*. It is pretty mundane, in fact – for it is simply the nature of our existence coming to know itself – a flowing in harmony with itself. But for the vast majority of us, this effortless, positive flow just does not happen often enough for us to consider it a potentially significant aspect of daily life.

Rather, we get used to experiencing a hellish dissonance between a self-centred, story-driven internal world, and a cold, heartless, nature-driven external world, and feel that there can be no escape from that all-pervading sense of dislocation.

Mindfulness and Zen philosophy change that view, however – by emphasising that if we want to be happier for longer, then we need to become more at ease with inevitable adversity – more peaceful and harmonious in our mortal organic being, so that the subtle, fine positivity of the flow state – of flowing in harmony with true nature, can be allowed to manifest within our lives more regularly, and perhaps for every moment of the rest of our days, even.

This enhanced broader flow requires some initial

effort in practice, though, since it is achieved through a more active, engaged, skilful approach to the use of our attention – that is, if we can even *remember* to pay attention skillfully, so that we can then actually *shift our primary focus* towards a more peaceful trajectory – away from anger, anxiety, mania, or boredom, for example, and *towards more positive congruence* with our wholesome civil values.

And that is not all, for on the level of our overall habit-driven life experience, sustained progress along the path towards more positive flow ultimately depends on whether both of those events – remembering to pay attention, and then skilfully shifting our attention, *happen often enough* – so that our mind and body enjoy any associated rewards and get on board the venture part-time, even, let alone full-time.

Thus, some Zen teachers talk of 'Great Determination' – of summoning a deep drive to endure life's inevitable hardships with dignity – perhaps along with a sense of existential urgency, so that one can persist with energised optimism through all the seasons of the heart. For in this way, the subconscious mind can get involved in a more powerful capacity – so that one more often remembers to shift attention away from chaos and towards peaceful harmony.

This latter step – shifting attention towards peaceful harmony, is the most essential and deeply profound step of them all, in fact, because whatever one pays attention to, *one becomes*.

For example, when enjoying the dramatic scenes in

an action movie, one's nervous system becomes highly activated as it follows along with the turbulence being depicted. However, if one were to change the channel to a nature documentary about fish swimming peacefully in the ocean, then one's nervous system would calm down.

So imagine, for a moment, that we could always have a huge tank full of graceful fish swimming next to us – when we are in a job interview, or when we are giving a presentation, or when meeting our future parents-in-law for the first time – that would help us to feel considerably calmer, would it not?

Well, a daily formal mindfulness practice allows for something similar to be available no matter where we are. In fact, it provides something even better – because we can come to recognise that we ourselves are graceful fish of sorts, since we are constantly 'swimming' through our ocean-like cosmos. And we can tune in to that aspect of our existence whenever we remember to do so, so that our daily affairs can go ahead *more swimmingly* – more fluidly and flowingly.

In this regard, mindfulness and Zen have, for thousands of years, provided people with a simple means of realising and releasing hidden potential – in order to excel, and thus succeed, when faced with adversity.

Therefore, this is not rocket science. Rather, it involves *merely choosing to pay conscious attention* to ever-available peace – by way of one's breathing, for example, or one's smoothly shifting physical balance.

For once inner peace is prioritised over inner turbulence (excessive mania or drama), one's mind gains a greater clarity of perception, and one's body has faster and more fluid motor responses.

And evolutionarily speaking, these are the kinds of cognitive and motile advantages that have governed survival or extinction, not to mention the laying down of foundations for the human civil societies that have grown to dominate this planet.

It is perhaps no wonder, then, that mindful approaches to staying alive have thus far survived book-burnings, invasions, spiritual reformations, and so forth, over the millennia and all over the world.

For by emphasising civil – 'heartful,' peaceful ethics, mindfulness is in harmony with the *Golden Rule* – a social principle found at the core of all long-lived communal philosophies; explicitly, the idea that one should treat others how one would wish to be treated – most often in a manner which is polite.

For no healthy person would hope for others to treat them violently, and so the essential ethical behaviour for any person who wishes to benefit long-term from a civilised society is *to continually and compassionately cultivate and maintain inner peace* – so that this equanimity may flow outwards and contribute to an ongoing engaged prosociality – so that many hands can continue to work together harmoniously in making staying alive a lighter task for everyone involved.

In this regard, the inner peace that mindfulness meditation generates has much to offer any human society anywhere in the world, and it has perhaps already supported, and continues to support and balance, myriad societies – as an element of the rituals of various religious denominations and yogas, for example – albeit under different brand names, of course.

At this point, then, hopefully enough has been said to adequately illustrate how secular mindfulness and traditional Chinese Zen overlap – so that the practical philosophical themes that will permeate the rest of this book are now clear – the notions, for example, that inner peace tends to be far more beneficial to ourselves and society than inner chaos, that both modern secular mindfulness and Zen aim to deliver that state of inner peace as efficiently and simply as possible in order to facilitate an increase in positive flow experiences, and that the core meditation practice that these disciplines share should be experienced first-hand, rather than just contemplated, in order to know it properly.

For the proof of the pudding is indeed in its eating. But how can we know which pudding to try, and how should it be eaten once we make our choice?

Thus, the chapters that follow aim to offer details regarding some different pudding options – some introductions to different traditional Chinese Zen arts, as well as their ideal serving suggestions – explanations illustrating how they are all precisely the same as western secular mindfulness meditation at their core.

It does not really matter, therefore, which art is practiced – whether one sits mindfully in silence, or paints a zen landscape, the final outcome will be the same, since it is all ultimately one path – one Dao. And yet, as another saying goes, 'there is more than one way to skin a cat.' So now let us move on to the mindfulness recipes without further ado.

2

YIQUAN KUNG FU: RESILIENCE

In all the martial arts systems all over the world, practitioners drill certain prescribed forms – characteristic shapes and movements, that are handed down to them by their teachers, except for in one martial art in particular, and its name is yiquan (pronounced "ee-tchwen").

For yiquan, which was distilled from the most practical and esoteric aspects of the Chinese martial arts known as xingyiquan (alleged to be mostly Daoist in origin), Shaolin kung fu (Zen Buddhist), and various others, *has no absolute form.*

In this regard, yiquan is the exception to the rule,

and yet, perfect posture is everything in yiquan. One could even say that posture is all the martial art is – a single, perfected resilient stance.

How can this be? Well, the Japanese Sōtō Zen master Shunryu Suzuki taught that the seated zazen meditation posture is itself enlightenment – it is empty of any describable form, and thus any selfishness – for it is buddha. It is just that when an unenlightened practitioner sits in that way, they feel that they – a someone, and therefore a self, is primarily *doing* the posture, rather than the stance arising automatically from their impersonal 'true nature' – from their *innate intelligence, or reflexive 'being.'*

And the same situation exists for yiquan posture training. For even though at first it can feel as if one is expanding and shaping one's body and mind oneself, as one becomes more proficient at the art, the expansive, robust shapes can be felt to arise reflexively from one's inherent intelligence – from the sophisticated biology that emerged from our planet, within our solar system, galaxy, and universe – all the way back to the raw dynamic energies of the big bang.

Before this aspect has been felt, or 'realised,' through direct experience, however, in order to try to make sense of what is occurring, the grasping mind tends to latch on to shallow surface patterns – assumed absolute forms, that revolve around our human world.

For when we are immersed within the unpredictable seas of change, the act of attaching our being to an intelligent agency – a self, an ego, or any rigid form or object, for that matter, tends to make us feel safer than having to face the alternative – namely, the more abstruse and ephemeral facets of our existential condition.

And yet, since in truth everything in our universe can be understood to be impermanent, how can any ego-driven, and thus rigid, act or form help us face constantly evolving adversity *at all times*?

It cannot truly help us – even if it seems to, and this is because, from a broader perspective, any notion of a permanent object – a rigid form, is out of harmony with the truth of what we see within and around us – that every thing, including our bodies, our opinions, memories, habits, and our state of wakefulness, is constantly changing in infinitely unpredictable and novel ways.

A form or formula of any sort, therefore – such as the concept of an essential self or a prescribed martial technique, even if it works for us perfectly the first one hundred times that we use it, can never be applied during a crisis in a universally reliable way. At some point the formula will surely fail, and that sudden impotence – that emptiness of practical value, could cost us dearly.

Before we can begin to gain any enthusiasm for accepting that bitter truth, however, we often have to find it out the hard way – by being forced to accept that absolute forms are ultimately empty of value – over and over again, until we finally surrender to such emptiness.

For example, a person who considers him- or herself to be an 'absolute winner' in life can never lose a competition without feeling *absolutely destroyed* – an experience which often causes them to flip to a new self-view that is just the opposite – that they must now be an absolute loser.

Similarly, martial artists who confidently learn formulated 'guaranteed to succeed' techniques find that those formulas do not always work when pressure tested in real life, and so they easily transition from being a martial arts know-it-all one moment, to an assumed ignoramus the next.

For there are an infinite number of variables always influencing a situation, and at every new moment those conditions are infinitely different from the moments before.

For example, an opponent may be taller, shorter, more flexible, thinner, or heavier than the people a martial artist usually trains with. Additionally, there could be a wall that is too close, the floor may be too slippery, or the practitioner might lack (for whatever momentary reason) the required energy or necessary relaxation to execute their favourite technique. Furthermore, it might be raining, there may be a friend or passer-by suddenly helping their opponent out, an unexpected or little understood weapon might be involved, or a practitioner could have so many different techniques in their repertoire to choose from that they feel 'log-jammed' – and so on and so forth.

Thus, the most resilient stance or posture that a martial artist can take up is one that is in harmony with (and can therefore source solutions from) the infinite ever-changing conditions of every fresh moment – a stance that can only be achieved through practicing *acceptance of 'what is,' or an 'open emptiness' – non-form*, as being the most potent 'form' of all.

For such an empty, and thus automatically fluid and expansive posture provides access to an unlimited amount of spontaneous creativity – the ability to be able to 'roll with the punches,' so to speak, whilst also being able to endure the inevitable storms that the impermanence of the universe whips up – storms such as the unavoidable loss of youth, health, and loved ones, before anyone even throws a spinning back-fist or whirlwind kick.

Because some people, no matter their having very caring and supportive friends and family members, are brutally knocked down by life itself. And this is often due to their attachment to rigid forms – their unwillingness to accept that everything is changing all of the time, making it impossible for them to harmonise and flow along with the universal law of impermanence – much to their detriment.

Thus, working artfully to negotiate constantly novel inevitable adversity is not only a subject for yiquan devotees and other martial artists to explore – it is relevant to every human being's existence.

We know this from the ever-increasing popularity of Mindfulness-Based Stress Reduction, for example, which aims to help people from all walks of life to more skilfully manage the human stress response within their ever-changing contexts – in the workplace, the family home, on the street, and so forth.

And so, yiquan, in being formless, is not necessarily even a martial art in the traditional sense, because despite its methodology proving very effective when employed within martial settings, it could just as easily be called a health preservation, rehabilitation, meditation, yoga, or strength enhancement system.

Thus, yiquan has been used in China to complement and enhance general athletic performances, and has also been successfully utilised in hospitals as a part of various treatments and rehabilitation programs – occurring in the decades before Jon Kabat-Zinn conducted his research into the healing effects of mindfulness meditation, even.

For during the middle of the twentieth century, a Japanese-educated Chinese doctor, called Yú YǒngNián (a direct student of Wáng Xiāngzhāi – 王芗斋, the founder of modern yiquan), had the inspiration to use yiquan 'standing yoga' in a Beijing hospital. And upon Dr. Yú running some simple scientific experiments to test how such postures affected the body, he obtained rather positive results, which he published in his book *Zhan Zhuang & the Search of Wu*.

And yet, what may be more surprising than those results is that during his lifetime, Dr. Yú ended up emphasising the health-maintenance aspects of yiquan more than its martial side. For even if yiquan is practiced only as a kind of yoga discipline, the outcome is indeed tangibly beneficial to a practitioner's health in every way.

In fact, such a health-focused perspective could be said to be closer to the heart of yiquan than combative push-hands is. Because no matter the primary reason for practicing the art, without a deeply caring attitude towards one's body as an initial premise, it will be difficult to persist in the prolonged stationary postures that are essential to its cultivation.

In this way, yiquan is again just like mindfulness

meditation – it builds its discipline on self-compassionate foundations, whilst utilising stationary posture work as an essential core practice.

However, even this self-compassionate stance remains ultimately formless, because, as we can discover from Richard Dawkins' book *The Selfish Gene*, for example, a deeply caring attitude towards ourselves and those whom we share our DNA with is not something that we need to conjure up and impose on our condition. It is, rather, inherent to all living organisms that are sophisticated enough to feel such an instinct.

Thus, when the expression of our genetic selfishness is not being overridden with entertaining mental forms that debase our true nature (what Dawkins calls 'memes'), it is reflexive for us to care for ourselves – to prioritise over other activities the future survival of our genetic material. It just becomes our present instinctive agenda.

Akin to formal Zen Buddhist teachings, therefore, yiquan immerses practitioners in a transcendent process that seeks to bypass any restrictive cultural trends – so that people may 'converse' directly with their self-interested, reflexively self-compassionate nature *through pure body language*. For this allows for any dysfunction being caused by the form-grasping mind to diminish – to the point, even, that the practitioner could achieve enlightenment, since, as a Zen saying goes, 'wherever concepts cannot enter, that is buddha.'

As a result, the first instruction that a yiquan teacher gives to a new student is for them to tune into and amplify the subtle sensations of life-affirming membrane-like elasticity that permeates every part of their body – a property that all living organisms are imbued with, in fact, and which manifests as a kind of expansive cellular springiness that represents a biological entity's natural intention to persist – to be tough yet flexible, and thus stand its ground with wholesome vigour and fluid adaptability.

This universal life-affirming reflexive compulsion, or 'will,' is called the 'Yì' (意) in Chinese, with yiquan thus roughly meaning 'natural intent pugilism.'

And in order to source its deeper essence, one can look to the natural environment outside of one's body, since the Yì is highly apparent in the structures of plants – in the way that branches and stems often spring back into their original upwards-and-outwards-reaching postures once any pressure that was bearing down upon them has been released.

And yet, again, even though this property has a label, life-affirming Yì is not some form that can be visualised in one's imagination and then applied to the body. Rather, it is a pure, direct *feeling* of lively vitality – of potent expansiveness or resilient fluid elasticity that medieval Chinese Zen masters equated with the flexibility of bamboo stems and pine tree branches – their limbs tending towards the heavens, constantly expanding outwards into the empty territories surrounding them.

Thus, yiquan martial artists practice standing and moving like deeply rooted trees that are being blown in the wind. But this is not an exercise in taking on the literal form of a tree in the same way that some animal styles of kung fu attempt to mimic every aspect of a particular creature. Instead, in yiquan, the goal is to take on the *formless, infinitely creative living spirit* – the perceived intent, of a resilient, springy, ever-expanding organic system (such as a tree or a tiger) that can remain upright and functional even when enduring considerable adversity.

In order for yiquan students to first source a feeling of the natural Yì, therefore, some yiquan teachers draw attention to the subtle springy sensations between their gently spread fingers. Others, meanwhile, akin to formal mindfulness meditation instructors, point to the sensations of the breathing process at the top of the belly – the reflexive movements of the tough yet springy diaphragm muscle, and how the belly rises and falls in response.

And once this inherently elastic, yet durable – *membranous*, property of the body becomes clearer, a practitioner may then look for its presence along the upright spine – especially at the back of the neck, by tucking the chin in a little and allowing the crown of the head to reach upwards. For as mindfulness and zazen instructors often say to their students, "the spine should be straight, but not too rigid, and yet also not too soft – just somewhere in between."

Because in this 'sweet spot,' where it is just right for us to thrive, a certain life-affirming springiness can indeed be detected – present all along the straightened spine, just like there is along a bamboo stem or blade of grass.

In fact, the same kind of robust springy feeling has been tuned to and utilised during traditional Indian yoga practices for millennia – in order to safely open up and increase the flexibility of the body.

The seated Zen meditation 'lotus posture' was born from this very tradition, even. For sitting with the feet folded onto the thighs was a standard ancient Indian yoga asana that was seemingly present within Vedic culture long before Gautama Buddha's followers appropriated it and carried it into China.

Since that time, however, a lot more empirical insight into biological systems has been achieved. And so, when looking at all of the above ancient wisdom from a more modern scientific perspective, we now know that what our human bodies hold in common with the bamboo stems and pine tree branches that the Zen masters of old appreciated so much, is the fact that they are all cellular structures, and that the inherent intention of every cell is to maintain its own pattern of organisation no matter the adversity that it meets.

Scientists have even given this process a name, which is *autopoiesis* – an automatic self-creation, that is always ongoing within every living organism.

Thus, in order to demystify yiquan somewhat, and indeed, to an extent, Zen meditation, and secular mindfulness along with it, we can see that the stances or postures employed by these arts are an attempt to amplify the autopoiesis that is inherent within the bodies that take on those postures – an amplification of the innate cellular spirit of living systems, or, as some Zen Buddhists like to call it, an accessing and embodying of an inherent intelligence – a Buddha Nature, or Inherent Enlightenment.

For autopoietic theory states that there exists a

cellular fractal symmetry of sorts that operates on at least three levels, or tiers, within the biological world. The first tier is that of single cells (the first autopoietic unit), then multicellular organisms (with their enclosing skins and inner tract surfaces operating like cell membranes), and thirdly, communities of multicellular organisms – organised 'cells' of like-minded beings (such as humans), which communicate and receive ideas between one another through 'social osmosis' – akin to when individual nerve cells interact and cooperate within a brain.

When secular mindfulness teachers seek to increase peoples' resilience by instructing them to open and expand their awareness, then (such as during a 'spacious awareness' meditation), this is, on a deeper level, in fact encouraging them to harmonise more with their innate cellular spirit – their inherent autopoiesis. For we now know, of course, that minds are generated by nervous systems, which in turn are constructed from nerve cells that serve all of life's autopoietic agenda – namely, a reflexive innate intention to expand to a fullness of being *in the spirit of a healthy swollen cell.*

We again find the same spirit in traditional Indian yoga, even, since the discipline seeks to open up a practitioner's body so that his or her circulation of energy and nutrition can improve – like when a single cell is expanded to its fullest extent so that its cytoplasm (which functions in a similar way to the blood supply of a multicellular organism) can more efficiently deliver resources to all of its components.

Yiquan postures are thus all formless in the respect

that nothing more is imposed during their practice than the directive to tune into and amplify *what is already present* – the wholesome cellular momentum occurring within the body, which is tangible as a subconscious always-on 'intent' just waiting there to be harnessed.

In order to saddle this potential during yiquan practice, therefore – so that it can be 'ridden into battle,' the conscious mind simply joins in with 'what is' – by harmonising with its own biological substrate via a cellular congruence.

And this immersion of one's whole being within reflexive cellular resilience is at first most effectively achieved by holding on to – resting within and upon, visualised cell-like 'balloons' of various sizes, because it allows the body's inherent autopoietic agenda to gain tangible extra support and power.

Once this stage has been mastered, however, then the yiquan practitioner can 'remove their stabilisers' – they can let go of and transcend the prescribed forms that they had previously been attached to. For by this time they will have gained a sense of whole body cellularity, and can just follow their wholesome, reflexively expansive bodily sensations.

This stage is the *true* yiquan.

And a similar method is used by formal mindfulness meditation practitioners, in fact – when, for example, after having first elongated their spines and tuned to their breathing according to a prescribed ideal, they seek to let go of that ideal – to trust their bodies to breathe themselves, thus allowing the waves of their expanding breath to carry them to a more peaceful, potent place – *automatically*.

What is more, this reflexive biological connection is made even clearer by Sōtō Zen meditation instructions – with zazen meditation students being told to allow their minds to rest within the expansion and contraction of their 'hara' – a region of the body that occupies the whole of the lower abdomen, and which is often depicted as a sphere embedded within the belly – like one large abdominal cell constructed from smaller cells.

In light of the above insights, it may even make intuitive sense, then, that the act of consciously tuning to and amplifying broader cellular feelings throughout the body will be 'enjoyed' by one's whole physiological system on multiple levels of biological functioning.

And in fact, after a suitable amount of yiquan practice, a kind of euphoria can indeed be detected throughout one's being – possibly due to the release of endorphins, in addition to the 'buzz' that accompanies a boosted metabolism.

For every yiquan practitioner finds that standing still in various postures for lengthy periods of time induces a ravenous appetite, as well as necessitates the consumption of large quantities of water – in order for one to not suffer from dehydration.

Furthermore, this interesting amplification of one's metabolism that yiquan posture training causes continues long after formal practice has finished – an aspect which harks back to stories of medieval tai chi masters, who, by practicing similar exercises to those found in yiquan, were able to drink unusually large quantities of wine without suffering from negative side effects – perhaps because their blood was being cleaned at a faster than normal rate.

In this way, an yiquan practitioner begins to gain an increased level of resilience – protection, against feelings of dis-ease, as well as intoxication and infection – by merely seeking to amplify their innate autopoiesis, and thus their in-built biological intention to expand and circulate blood as freely and abundantly as possible.

But this is not all, for once one moves into the martial training aspect of yiquan, one may also benefit from an increased level of toughness when enduring blunt physical blows during a conflict – due to the fact that when the cellular springiness particular to such arts as yiquan and tai chi is manifested throughout the whole bodily frame – from the balls of the feet, to the hands, and the crown of the head, it can be used as a kind of shock absorber for impacts (a property called 'iron shirt' in traditional Chinese kung fu).

The cellular Yì thus becomes an incredibly valuable resource for martial artists, since skillful warriors often like to deliver sudden sharp whacks and yanks to the arms and weapons of their opponents – in order to cause them to flinch and freeze up, and therefore momentarily stun, distract, and imbalance them.

As far as competent yiquan practitioners are concerned, however, such stun tactics merely serve as a kind of massage – as the yiquan warrior's frame absorbs impacts akin to a water-filled balloon that is rooted to the ground like a tree.

Nevertheless, an yiquan fighter does not intend to just stand there and take blows like a punchbag – far from it. When conflict is unavoidable, they seek, rather, to use offense as the best defense. And this is, yet again, accomplished by way of their deeply rooted stance – their whole body intra-connectivity.

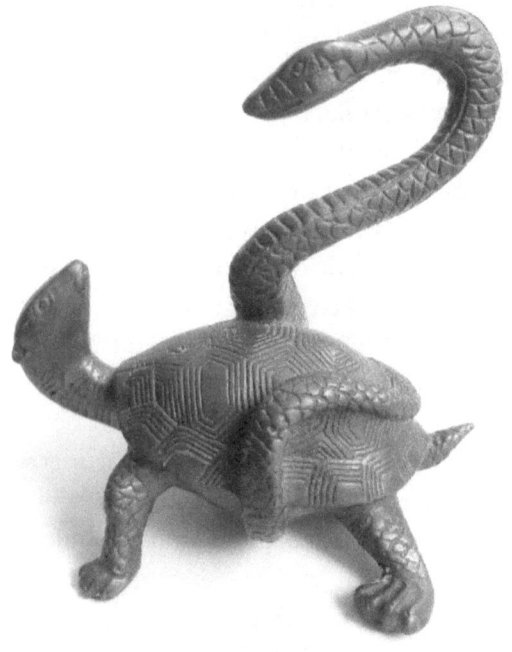

A bronze sculpture of a turtle entwined with a snake – an ancient Chinese symbol representing the highest martial arts path.

For the yiquan pugilist can use their highly stable lower body to allow their torso to rapidly coil and whip – to issue explosive strikes that spiral from the ground upwards, should they need to, all the while maintaining their tough resilience via the same stance.

In this respect, yiquan's defensive strategy is not to

become like a turtle that hides in its shell, but rather to combine a turtle with a snake – *to be robustly grounded and tough, whilst simultaneously assertive – frighteningly fluid.*

Because yiquan does not view violence as some kind of game – some cultural art form or sport to celebrate and indulge in. Rather, it sees such activity as risking an untimely death, and therefore needs to be dealt with as quickly and authoritatively as possible, since fighting only causes additional chaos – disharmony.

That being so, violence of all sorts does come naturally to uneducated humans, and so it is a factor that will always be present in human societies – especially amongst children.

Thus, the arrival of violence in one's world must be accepted to a degree – given its due recognition, with mindful grounded attention, so that it may be most effectively mastered – constrained, and without any entertaining displays, or glory in victory.

For it is this very noble intent that allows for a fuller expansion in mind and body to occur, in fact – as it empowers all life to flourish more openly and vigorously – confidently, with wholesome, flexible inner resilience.

And these resilient aspects of yiquan can even be observed to manifest within the world of secular mindfulness – but usually only on the level of the mind.

For example, some experienced mindfulness meditators report that they have gained an increase in their ability to take heavy mental knocks whilst remaining centred and grounded, and to be able to recover instantly, even – just like a bamboo stem flicking upright after heavy snow falls off.

In this respect, then, the human mind could be said to be generally 'cell-shaped' – to be operating according to the spirit of a cellular structure, in the sense that it has the inherent intent to expand to its fullest extent – in order to remain at optimum functionality, rather than become narrowed due to all of the inevitable adversity that it encounters, and thus afflicted and weak-spirited.

Yiquan, mindfulness, and Zen meditation are therefore all just practices that highlight and champion this natural intent of body and mind to expand and endure, so that a greater physical and mental resilience may be facilitated – a greater ease of being in and of the world.

And such a condition is mainly achieved through sustaining prolonged, relatively still postures – no matter the modality being practiced, since standing or sitting can both achieve the same aims – as the body remains in place with a sense of noble dignity, like a deeply rooted Bodhi tree that is reaching outwards and upwards with potent, lively, flexible vitality.

For by way of such posture work, a harmony between the cellularity of mind and body can be most efficiently facilitated – as a congruent flow, which is to be maintained as they move together through space and inter-be as one whole, integrated, tough yet flexible, autopoietic unit.

However, this is still not the whole story – there are yet more benefits for those willing to put in the hard work. Because yiquan's resilience not only manifests as a capacity to withstand some sudden heavy impacts and generate explosive power, but also as an elegant *organisational flexibility – a fluidity of biological being.*

For cells, in addition to enclosing and protecting an inner space by way of maintaining a durable membrane, *constantly metabolise and regenerate themselves* from within that space – to the point that mutations in their genetic foundations may take place, even.

Such mutations cause the cells' autopoietic pattern of organisation to change – beneficially, benignly, or catastrophically, and if new survival benefits are indeed gained, then we say that the cell has more successfully adapted to its environment – it has evolved.

But each adaptation is never a rigid, finalised form, because the environment is always in flux, making adaptability *a universal ongoing necessity* of primary importance in the lives of all organisms.

It is this very practical and realistic survival need, therefore – *to be able to evolve with the times – to constantly adapt to any new situation*, that ultimately explains why yiquan (and the autopoietic Zen mind that it originates from) *has no prescribable form* – no absolute pattern of organisation to emulate or champion beyond its inherently fluid expansiveness.

Thus, when Master Shunryu Suzuki was asked by one of his students to reduce Zen Buddhism to a single phrase, he is alleged to have replied, "everything changes."

He said this, it seems, because it is impossible to use any rigid form or prescribed posture to adequately describe the process of flowing in harmony with an ever-changing universe.

Therefore, behind the seemingly still surface of a Zen posture is a potent infinite fluidity – a dynamic, relentlessly creative *intent*, that is sourced directly from our biological nature – an intention to *intelligently persist* by constantly adapting to circumstances with robust vigour.

Yiquan practitioners must thus eventually let go of any idea of absolute physical posture or stance, and instead manifest a condition that originates from beyond form – via an absolutely *formless, and thus empty, spacious, potent* form that emanates from the domain of raw, dynamic, ever-changing nature itself.

This is the most powerful ally any warrior could ever hope to gain – a trusty steed upon which to fly into battle, that is nothing less than the potency of the whole universe from which he or she automatically appears.

The legendary Daoist sage LaoTzu therefore states in the very first line of his book, the *DàoDéJīng*, 'there is no one absolute prescribable Way.' And this is the essential characteristic of all true Ways – all true paths to enlightenment. For they are empty of any rigid concept – any calculated formulas or clever tricks.

Instead, they are just like pure, flowing, ever-changing water – ready to spread throughout any vessel, and thus adapt to its shape – to survive robustly in any ecological niche that they are poured into. And that seems to sum up the resilient essence of yiquan, Zen practice, mindfulness, and this life process of ours rather well.

3

YIQUAN KUNG FU: FLUIDITY

During yiquan push-hands practice, two cellular structures are attempting to move through one another – just like when two trees' branches meet in a dense forest.

As their bodies clash, they test their deep-rooted wills to survive – their respective intentions to persist in their uprightness, their limbs reaching out – expanding into vast spaciousness, in order to explore and control any potent territory that is within reach.

Another way of describing this process is to say that yiquan practitioners test their 'philosophies of pure presence' – their respective harmonies with the true forces of nature, all the way down to their roots.

For encountering opposition – all the random obstacles and storms that arrive as a natural part of life, is inevitable for every person on our planet.

And in the same way that storms cause trees to proverbially grow deeper roots, as yiquan push-hands practitioners apply pressure to one another's fully expanded existential structures, they enjoy considerable personal benefits, since they receive a deep internal massage that penetrates not only into their bodies, but also their minds.

This only occurs, however, if their yiquan standing posture practice – their foundational discipline within which they seek to fully expand their minds and bodies, and thus their 'rooting' in general (as it is referred to in the *Tai Chi Classics*), has been adequately established beforehand, because otherwise they will soon enough be sent hurtling across the training space.

In this regard, there is a considerable overlap between yiquan and formal mindfulness meditation, in fact, for both disciplines require regular adequate investment in daily posture practice as a preparation for meeting inevitable adversity.

Once this investment has been made, though, then there naturally arises the reflexive capacity to transform the struggles of life into additional personal gain – to use adversity as a source of ongoing increased sustenance, and effortlessly so.

The Japanese martial art of aikido, which has a seated Zen meditation component to it, is famous for this very ideal, even – often being described as a martial art that aims to neutralise an opponent's negative energy by fluidly and efficiently using their aggressive force against them.

And coincidentally (or perhaps not), before Jon Kabat-Zinn had conducted some of the first formal scientific research into the healing effects of mindfulness meditation, he had been a keen aikido practitioner. What is more, he would even go on to use practical examples from aikido when teaching mindfulness at his stress-reduction clinic, as well as when giving meditation advice in his famous book on secular mindfulness, called *Full Catastrophe Living*.

This was nothing particularly new, though, for it has been common throughout history for mindfulness teachings to make references to the world of martial arts – since the path to enlightenment itself, as taught by Gautama Buddha of the Shakya clan, has often been referred to as 'the path of the warrior.'

In the Buddhist text *The Dhammapada*, for example, Shakyamuni Buddha states that the person who defeats their self – their ego, is more victorious than the person who defeats a thousand people a thousand times in battle.

Thus, authentic Zen kung fu begins with turning towards our ego – our rigid notion of self (what Buddhist's often describe as Mara), in order to 'spar' with its anti-social spirit, and in the process get to know its cunning tricks and propaganda.

For after practicing sufficiently in this way, we may then be able to conquer, or master, our egos enough so that we can reap the rewards of increased prosociality – a benefit which can include a more vigorous intra-cellular cohesion occurring within one's body (one's internal multicellular community), as well as within any of one's external communities.

In this light, then, a Zen battle of any sort ultimately takes place within a practitioners mind, and is never won through the warrior primarily wielding violence. Rather, victory is achieved via a channeling of heroic saintliness – a cohesive warm-hearted loving kindness, which in turn facilitates the grounded rooting, dynamic potential, and creative intelligence necessary for the Zen warrior to prevail.

Of course, this cohesive warm-heartedness is not the default mode that we are born into. Instead, we are born 'red in tooth and claw' – reflexively inhumane, and it becomes the responsibility of our parents and broader social institutions to educate us into a more sophisticated condition.

We never lose that inhumane potential, however – we just keep it dormant, and it can come to the fore whenever we want.

This means that we are inherently *socio-economically fluid* – we can cooperate altruistically with others one moment, and then cheat them selfishly the next, all depending on our momentary whims – our gut instincts.

For as Richard Dawkins' book, *The Selfish Gene*, points out – in harmony with Lao Tzu's first chapter of *DàoDéJīng*, in fact, humans are neither inherently evil nor saintly – *we are not locked into any one way of persisting.*

Rather, we are efficiency-driven opportunists – we look for the most direct route to our destination, just like a stream flowing down a mountain under the influence of gravity.

And yet, many hands cooperating intelligently of course make lighter work of any task, meaning that in nature, no matter the organisms concerned, prosociality tends to trump antisociality – it tends to provide us with the most direct route down the economic mountain to more abundant resources.

That is not to say that parasitism cannot deliver benefits to 'lone wolves,' of course. Indeed it can, and often does. But if an individual is *habitually closed to honest cooperation, then they severely limit their options* – they can easily lose out in significant ways further down the road, since, as the saying goes, 'there is rarely any honour among thieves.'

For more sophisticated humans, however, we have opportunities to cultivate a more genuinely prosocial, equal, habitually humane existence – a predominantly virtuous stance, which can empower us above and beyond any parasitic approach – because there is true honour involved, true honesty, and thus deeper trust.

Therefore, in order to meet the world in the most potent, intelligent way, we need to be constantly *open to all* socio-economic strategies – the 'low,' or 'narrow' (which comes naturally to us – such as when we prioritise our own family's needs over another's), as well as the 'high,' or 'broad' – the charitable, *which must be consciously cultivated*.

Once a warrior can remain constantly open, then – accepting of the inevitably antisocial approaches, *as well as the need to proactively cultivate prosocial approaches*, they tend to manifest the most practical condition of mind and body – a balanced 'Middle

Way,' when faced with adversity. For they have the most tools – the most potency and intelligence, at their disposal.

Lao Tzu even seems to refer to this truth in Chapter 28 of his *DàoDéJīng*, which begins as follows:

"Know your raw masculine power,

but stand with your gentle feminine power,

acting as a humble conduit for the potency of the universe."

知	其	雄
Zhī	Qí	Xióng
realise	one's	imposing masculinity

守	其	雌
Shǒu	Qí	Cí
abide by	one's	gentle femininity

为	天	下	溪
Wéi	Tiān	Xià	Xī
acting as	the heavens'	subservient	channel

Such a flexible, yet highly potent, condition of being is necessarily marked by a spontaneous yet philosophically congruent fluid adaptability – like a writhing snake, *or a Chinese dragon*, which can allow a person to confidently benefit from both antisocial and prosocial situations as and when they arise.

This is not to say that maintaining such a condition will always triumph, however. Rather, it just tends to be the most robust potential solution under most circumstances – and especially so when all else between competing sides is equally matched. For although we cannot control the world around us very readily, we *can* relatively easily gain control over, or perhaps 'allegiance' from, our inner domain – should we want to.

Thus, underlying the external, visible form of a true Zen martial arts practice, there is always an echo of a deeper, more powerful inner discipline – the practice of spontaneously adapting to the unavoidable impermanent conditions of the universe – a deep-set intention to maintain one's internal integrity as one goes about one's ever-changing daily life.

For beyond us very occasionally having to fend off hungry tigers (or their human equivalent), *our most frequent battles are fought against our anxious selves* – against any negative, contractive mental responses to representations of the truth that, at some point, our discernible being must completely disintegrate – must be lost to the entropy of the universe.

The outcomes of all Zen battles are ultimately decided, therefore, by whether the practitioner, when faced with their constant, necessary loss of time and energy – their unavoidable mortality, swells up with dynamic potency in celebration of their ongoing life, or instead shrivels up with fear regarding what they assume could happen in the future.

So no matter whether we are sat meditating, practicing yoga, or playing yiquan push-hands, we can learn rather quickly that in order to win at these 'games of life' – to not be defeated by the inevitable stormy forces of chaos in the most untimely way, we need to *stay fluid in body and mind, and accept* – as best we can, via a pervading light-hearted, unattached 'can do' optimism, what cannot be changed.

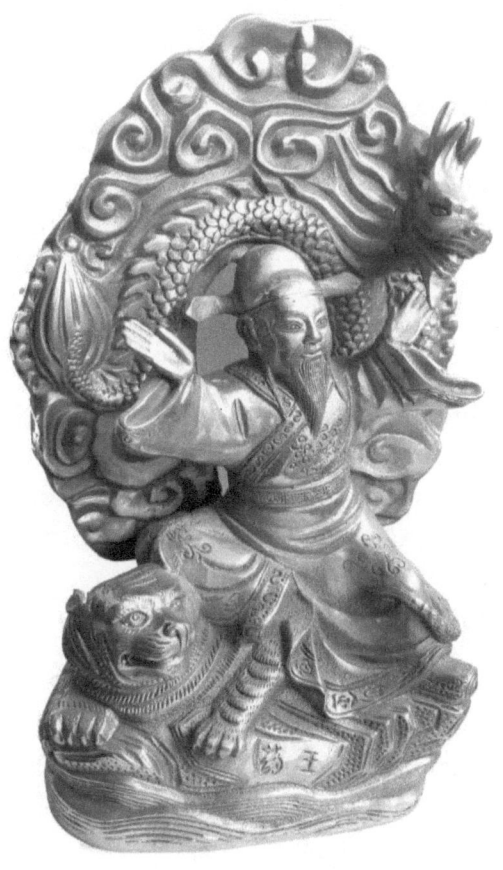

A bronze sculpture of the traditional Chinese 'Medicine King,' called Yàowáng, sitting atop a tiger, and 'crowned' by a dragon.

We must accept, for example, the natural, necessary loss of youth, health, and our elegant nervous systems that deliver so much joy and economic benefit as we pass through our lives.

And such fluid acceptance of nature is not a mere mental statement – it is not simply repeating to ourselves the words "it's okay." For in its most practical form, acceptance occurs *beyond our logical faculties and the symbols that we manipulate*, in the purely physical domain of bioeconomic activity – a realm of abstract yet highly tangible bodily sensations.

Thus, the Chinese Buddhist *Heart Sutra* states, 'Within the deep channel of wisdom beyond wisdom... ....go beyond the beyond,' inferring that we must go beyond the mere idea of 'beyond' – to a domain of wisdom that exists beyond the mere idea of 'wisdom,' or any other concepts, such as 'self,' 'me,' or 'others.'

As a result of recognising this potential, Zen and mindfulness practitioners therefore intend to relax their bodies as much as possible, whilst maintaining an expanded, alert, upright posture – an openness to truthful experience, that is arriving from beyond concepts.

This practice was apparently described by the first patriarch of Zen and Shaolin kung fu, Bodhidharma, as 'going forth into thusness' – a going forth into acceptance of 'what is,' fluid impermanence – flux, with invigorated enthusiasm.

Such an optimised condition of existence may also be called conserving one's adaptability – as coined by the authors of the theory of autopoiesis in their book *The Tree of Knowledge: The Biological Roots of Human*

Understanding. For during the evolution of species on our planet, genomes that maintained their potential to adapt to climate fluctuations, diseases, and so on, were the ones that tended to survive mass extinctions.

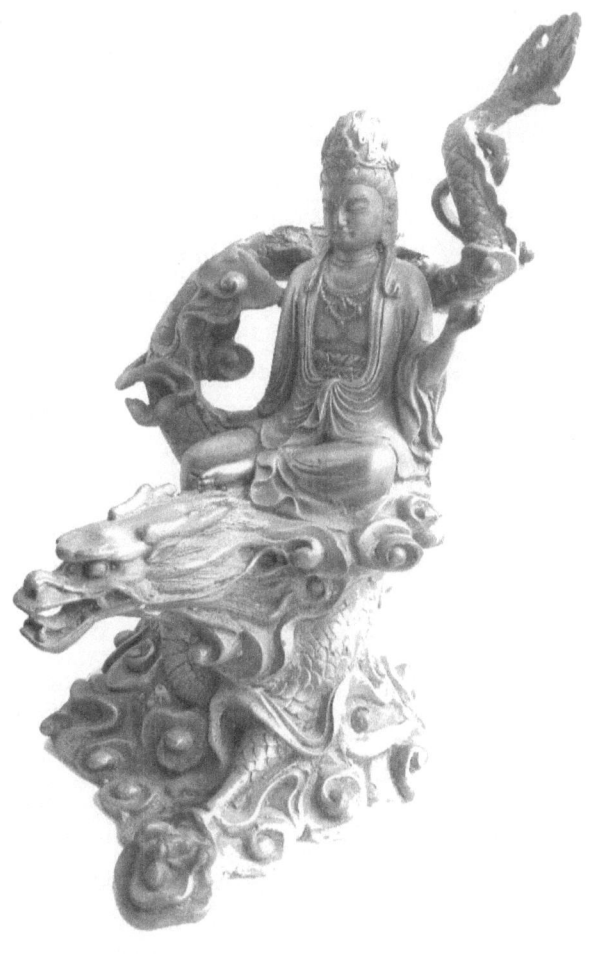

A bronze sculpture of GuānYīn, the Chinese 'Goddess of Compassion,' peacefully riding a traditional Chinese dragon.

Thus, it may be of no surprise to hear that the *Tai chi Classics* describe the ideal condition of body as one where if a small feather were to alight on one's finger, it would set one's whole physical structure in motion – just like ripples of disturbance sent out across the surface of a perfectly still lake, in order that one may spontaneously adjust and rebalance oneself in the most intelligent and efficient way.

And such martial insight, or practical philosophical posturing, was, no doubt, what prompted the late kung fu movie star Bruce Lee to famously advise us, 'be like water, my friend' – an admonishment that he intended not only for the body, but also for the mind.

For this wisdom of conserving one's fluid adaptability is nothing new to people in China – it goes back thousands of years, with LaoTzu stating in the *DàoDéJīng*, 'the Dao resembles water' – a proposition that the true Way of operating in harmony with the natural universe must always be inherently watery, because nature itself is relentlessly fluid.

This insight was also present in the West during LaoTzu's time, even, since one of the first Greek philosophers, Thales of Miletus, declared that water was the ultimate source – the *arche*, from which all things arose.

And after this, Heraclitus famously offered that one cannot step into the same river twice, because the whole universe is continually flowing and changing.

But such wisdom emphasising universal impermanence was to be extrapolated still even further by the ancient Greeks – by an eccentric Heraclitean philosopher, called Cratylus, who went on to became one of Plato's teachers, in fact.

For Cratylus argued that if all objects are constantly changing, then the foot that repeatedly steps into Heraclitus' river cannot be the same foot from one moment to the next.

Thus, Heraclitus' most distinguished disciple finally concluded that all spoken labels – such as 'river' and 'foot,' are inherently flawed – due to the fact that they attempt to freeze the ever-changing forms that they refer to.

Instead of using words to philosophise, then, Cratylus was alleged to have preferred to simply move his finger – to more safely manipulate and relate the tangible, physical phenomena of the practical universe via pure body language. This is so that he would not commit any logical fallacies, and could thus more consistently penetrate the truth of nature.

For by more directly manifesting his functional wisdom in this purely physical way, *it could be relied upon with utmost confidence when he was under significant pressure.*

And this is precisely the kind of confidence that yiquan push-hands testing builds – since, as mentioned earlier in this book, the ultimate proof of our ability to respond to life's pressures with the most beneficial 'recipe' is in 'the eating of the pudding' – in how our overall posture of mind and body fares when the storms roll in.

Therefore, in order that a yiquan practitioner is ready at any time to competently 'roll with the punches,' they seek peaceful refuge in the fluidity of 'what is,' and in precisely the same way that mindfulness and Zen practitioners do – they source and champion their biological predisposition to elegant, prosocial, adaptive, sophisticated solutions (as embodied during relaxed yet robustly-held meditative postures), so that their resilient response is effortlessly instant when needed.

Perhaps unsurprisingly, then, even though yiquan, being a martial art, is of course more physically dynamic than seated meditation, at least thirty percent of an intensive daily yiquan practice regimen is spent standing still – standing like a tree or a wooden post. For this seems to be the most efficient way to finely tune one's body and mind to the subtle yet tangibly positive intentions of one's true nature – to the natural cellular impulse to 'frolic' in harmony with the universe's organic beauty.

And only after this tuning has been completed effectively enough can one's fine 'symphony' be shared with the world – by one flowing along congruently with the reflexive cellular metabolism within and around one's being, thus reinforcing and amplifying that very metabolism via one's wholesome movements.

The competent yiquan practitioner never loses sight, therefore, of a sense of wholesome, springy, adaptive, flowing cellularity – a sense of our dynamic autopoiesis, which may be called 'an eternal spring within one's heart,' permeating one's whole body and mind.

And so, just like for mindfulness and Zen practices, yiquan is ultimately a state of attentiveness – a condition of being or presence, a paying attention to, and amplification of, the true nature that is always within and around us.

In martial contexts, this results in one's bodily frame moving reflexively like a dragon – swimming and frolicking in the watery ever-changing cosmos, which can look like a dance of sorts (a yiquan 'health dance' (called JiànWǔ in Chinese)), that is very beautiful at times.

And yet, as mentioned in the previous chapter, this dance has no *absolute* form, and therefore cannot be absolutely analysed, emulated, or prescribed. Rather, it is all simply a product of one's innate physiological mechanics being liberated by an expanded mental and physical posture – a conscious commitment to dwelling beyond such conceptual forms as 'swimming dragon,' 'wisdom,' 'dance,' 'beauty,' or 'being beyond objects,' even. For there is no time or need for thinking. there is only congruence with ever-present true nature to be tuned to – sourced, and then appreciated.

In this way, yiquan martial training postures and moving exercises attempt to harness the exact same fluid and expansive intent that seated zazen meditation does, but with the practitioner's limbs rotated in various other directions.

And this detail is of no impact to the spiritual outcome of yiquan training, in fact. For *the ultimate posture is in the natural mind* – in its wholesome autopoiesis, where it is free from any divisive forms that obscure the seamless, dynamic wholeness of our being.

Thus, if the body can sit or move without mentally grasping at this or that – in harmony with its fluid autopoiesis, flowing along with its sociable cellular spirit – its inherent prosocial potential that cares for all cells, multicellular organisms, and communities of multicellular organisms alike, then buddha can be felt, no matter what change in body shape is occurring.

Because such a noble 'buddha mind' – our soft yet upright, fully accepting expansive mind, flows in harmony with the undeniable truth of impermanence – the truth that even our very pattern of organisation, our DNA, can mutate and become something different, no matter our ego-driven preferences for any other truth.

The act of competently flowing in harmony with our true nature is therefore just a matter of noticing – *tuning to and feeling*, its dynamic presence within us, and following along with its graceful yet powerful momentum – akin to, as the Buddha states in the *Daruka-khandha Sutta: The Log*, a log that floats down a river until it becomes indistinguishable from the river's inherent fluidity – the flux of all objects, with river, log, and self, becoming *just one spirited momentum*.

For our whole structure may freeze like ice, expand flexibly like a bubble, turn, twist, and spin like a whirlpool, and even sweep forward with great energy – leaping up like an ocean swell, and crashing down like a tsunami, all depending on what is required in order to conserve our wholesome cellularity.

And such fluid potential is mentioned, yet again, in LaoTzu's *DàoDéJīng* – advising us that we should emulate water as often as possible, because it delivers ungraspability, and can therefore help us to more easily escape any overwhelming force – so that we may live to fight another day.

And yet, we have an even better source of natural fluidity available for inspiration, perhaps – a source that is always to hand no matter our climate or elevation, and which is finer than the water in the most pure and peaceful lake.

It is what we today call the autopoietic mind, as it manifests right here, right now – *a relentless stream of consciousness and unconsciousness*, which flows along in congruence with all of the cellular processes on our planet – in the form of our fundamental existential intent to adapt to conditions as we face inevitable change.

In order to flow along with it in perfect harmony, however, yiquan, Zen, and mindfulness teach us that we must open up – surrender, to our reflexively dynamic, creative, and thus highly potent inherent nature – so that we may more intelligently, elegantly – fluidly, gain victories over adversity.

4

YIQUAN KUNG FU: LISTENING

LaoTzu states, in his book *DàoDéJīng*, that it is the empty space within a window, a wheel, or a cup that makes it useful, and therefore all utility depends upon emptiness.

This idea has great value for a mindfulness meditation practitioner, because it reminds them that it is not a busy mind full of this or that which creates true productivity in their lives. Rather, it is a clear, uncluttered ongoing view of what is most important that benefits them the most – a space for new, strong, stable organic growth to happen in its own time.

For true insight and fresh solutions do not tend to arrive from the domain of conscious emulation and tailoring, because those activities involve the manipulation of already created objects. Instead, profound 'aha moments' – spontaneous, fresh realisations, and thus fresher approaches to a problem, most often occur when we are not busying ourselves with the details of finding such solutions – when we are taking a bath, for example, or out walking in the park.

And so, this creative process, fed by our inherent 'always on' reflexive intelligence, can be trusted to provide us with useful solutions as and when possible – only, that is, if we can successfully maintain the necessary amount of mental space and therefore *a suitable level of emptiness within our being*.

Sometimes, even just meeting a situation with emptiness itself is the best solution – just letting something go. But how can the beauty of that response ever be discovered if we are always so 'high on' (and therefore often addicted – attached to, and full of) the mental objects swashing around in our heads?

For example, a famous Zen story tells of a proud university professor who visited a Zen master in order to obtain a clear verbal description of Zen practice. The master invited the professor in for a cup of a tea, and as he prepared the beverage for his guest, he continued pouring until the liquid flowed up and over the sides of the cup.

The professor, feeling shocked and a little upset, asked what the purpose of such an act was. The Zen master replied that the professor's mind, being so full of descriptions and theories about the world, was just like the cup – it was overflowing uselessly.

In this way, the master helped the professor to realise that in order to get a grip on the true practical quality of Zen, his mind firstly needed to become somewhat empty. For after that, his mind would have more utility – it would have more clarity to perceive the true nature of his present conditions directly.

And exactly this idea is applied during yiquan push-hands practice – or indeed within any Zen arts context. Because once we can more competently comprehend our situation – once we know where we truly are, then we can make the most practical, stable, productive progress towards where we would like to be or go.

This was stated more succinctly by the ancient Chinese military strategist Sun Tzu, in his book *The Art of War*, as 'know your enemy.'

Thus, when a competent yiquan practitioner connects arms combatively with an opponent (no matter whether via their forearm, or with a weapon), if they do not choose to immediately deflect the arm or explode forward (due to already having read the situation with confidence), they instead expand both body and mind and drop into emptiness (YìWúYì – 意无意; 'intent of no intent') – as best they can.

Afterwards, they just listen and flow with present conditions, the whole of their being becoming open – receptive, as they scan for information that communicates their opponent's (or their own) weaknesses – like a doctor carefully checking a patient's health.

For as the saying goes, 'knowledge is power,' and so as soon as they identify some object that is separated from its background – detached from its existential substrate, they may then find its centre of gravity – its beating heart, and manipulate it as they wish.

In this respect, carefully exploring the fluidity of the present moment is a kind of default activity for yiquan push-hands practitioners – as they swim like dragons within the seas of change, until they discover a 'dragon ball' to play with, some aggregate of unanchored energy – an aloof, ungrounded piece of rigid (Jiāng – 僵) untempered ego, either within their opponent's body, or within their own. Then, akin to a masseur who encounters a knot of tension, they now have something to work with.

In order to manifest this process successfully, a competent yiquan push-hands practitioner must therefore empty themselves of ego – they must let go of any desire to win, so that they *can* win – so that they can remain truly fluid, and thus spontaneous and adaptable – their coiling limbs, spine, and rooted feet passing cloud-like through the 'sky' of their awareness.

And a mindfulness or Zen meditator similarly intends to let go of all conscious self-ish objectives – by allowing thoughts to simply come and go like drifting clouds.

Such an empty, receptive condition of nervous system and body is not some lofty or 'expert' state of existence, though. In fact, it can be experienced instantly by any person – right now, even – by seriously contemplating a traditional Zen riddle, or koan (GōngÀn – 公案).

One could choose, for example, 'What is the sound of one hand clapping?'

Immediately, upon taking up this challenge with one's whole being, the mind is sent into an emptiness, as one's cognitive system expands – looking in all directions for an answer. And this response, or infinitely open 'trance' *is* the answer!

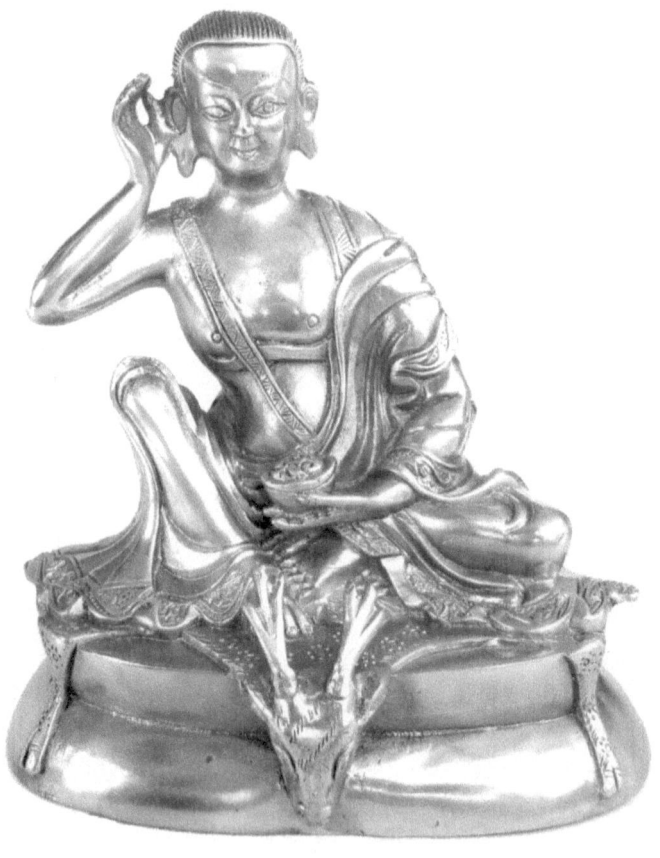

A bronze sculpture of the Tibetan Buddhist yogi Milarepa, who is listening to the song of Nature – the Absolute Truth.

For no matter the illogicality of the question, it is the resultant open, receptive state of mind that is the practical truth – the utility, of Zen practice.

And yet, if a verbally communicated response to the riddle is required by a Zen teacher, then this is not a problem, since the empty stance that pondering this kind of conundrum creates will at some point deliver a spontaneous *context-specific* momentarily-communicable insight – something which can only be arrived at after such an empty condition of body and mind has been maintained for long enough.

In the case of yiquan push-hands practice, however, the Zen riddle can be, 'How can one achieve martial victory by surrendering?'

And a correct yiquan-oriented 'answer' to this question is communicated through pure body language – when the practitioner has physically and mentally surrendered to the true nature that unites both combatants, allowing him or her to remain physically and mentally rooted even though considerable dynamic pressure has been applied to their martial posturing.

For such an outcome is indeed something which can only be achieved by surrendering to one's natural, biological cellular intention to remain fluid and expanded – spontaneously adaptable and wholesome, through a proactive emptying out of antisocial, divisive ego-driven assumptions.

In this light, then, the practitioner that 'wins' the martial victory is not even present as an ego or self. For ultimately it is just nature that 'wins.' And yet, since the very same nature is present in both the winner and the loser, how can a singular nature even achieve such a dualistic condition?

Thus, a victorious competent yiquan practitioner feels his or her achievement arriving from somewhere beyond their sense of self and self-ishness – from beyond their conception of nature, even. It just arrives effortlessly – as if by magic, from a place of formlessness – of potent, fluid, unified emptiness.

In order to be empowered in the above way through mindfulness, Zen, or yiquan, therefore, first one must be empty enough to receive that empowerment – one's nervous system must be cleared of obstructions, so that the ever-changing fluid truth can arrive from beyond the limited domain of frozen, rigid concepts.

The mindful 'warrior sage' thus flows receptively – openly and emptily, with the conditions of the present moment as they come and go – just like a cat waiting patiently, relaxed, yet highly attentively, at a mousehole. This is so that when the mouse makes his speedy exit – like when a mountain peak suddenly appears from swirling clouds, it may be pounced upon and grasped – captured, in order that the 'hunter' may receive a nourishing reward.

And although such posturing can be employed for good or for bad, it is also a fact that a cold heart is icy – hard, rigid, and therefore never as fluid and flowing as that of a warm-hearted person.

As a result, we can have faith in our reflexively prosocial, accommodating dimension. For in the same way that streams and rivers carve through intimidating mountains as they continually flow down to an ocean, the softness of an easy-going, civil, fluid state of being, if sustained, will always eventually overcome the hard, grim, contractedness of stony hearts.

Thus, no matter whether one encounters an emotional knot in one's stomach, or a friend's contracted shoulder muscle fibres, or a seemingly immovable giant, by maintaining a constant dynamic flow of being – akin to coiling ocean waves or serpents smoothly moving around and against any obstruction, one may eventually exploit its weaknesses – any inevitable inherent fissures or fractures in its stony condition, and emerge victorious.

For *every natural object is flawed* – meaning that even the most formidable dam or fortress can be undermined and caused to crumble to pieces – and without any effort on the part of the flowing warrior, since it feels good, congruent, effortlessly harmonious to *be* that more warm-hearted, melting, adaptable, and therefore 'superior' person.

In this light, then, when expecting to encounter unavoidable adversity, no matter whether one practices mindfulness, Zen, or yiquan, all one needs to do is to perfect one's wholesome posture on a daily basis, let go into fluidity, and after that just listen – with any spontaneous solutions naturally arising and fading away within one's infinite sky-like awareness – to the sound of one hand clapping.

5

ZEN CALLIGRAPHY: TRACE

It is said that upon looking at a piece of traditional Chinese calligraphy, one sees the writer. But what exactly is it that one can see about them?

Well, in the case of their brushwork, we can observe the way that they interacted with the brush – how they danced along with it as it twisted and turned. And due to the fineness of the medium – the water-like fluidity of the ink, we can even detect how peaceful the writer's heart was during that dance, since the calligrapher's level of inner peace is intimately connected with their finger movements and therefore the trace – the strokes, that their brush leaves behind.

For Zen and mindfulness are all about our

relationship with nature – how we interact with and respond to our environments, and thus the *way* in which we approach the universe around us.

In this light, then, it is necessary for a Zen calligrapher to be able to communicate *The Way* reliably and tangibly, and they do, when their art is performed correctly – when they can relate mindfully to all conditions as they arrive.

This is not a particularly complex procedure in and of itself, and yet, in addition to being mindful of the conditions of one's body and mind, it must also involve – incorporate, the properties of the calligraphy brush, the ink, the calligraphy piece as it develops over time, as well as the rest of the world – the entire existential space within which one persists.

As a result, such a calligraphy practice can be used as a mindfulness or Zen path in its own right, which is an idea that is still widely recognised in the Far East today.

For example, the Japanese Sōtō Zen master Shunryu Suzuki used to enjoy creating Zen calligraphy pieces endlessly – to the extent, even, that he would sometimes resist his schedule and continue writing.

However, after rendering his calligraphy works with such a resisting heart, Suzuki would see within his deposited strokes his own stubbornness – a level of disharmony, which threatened to undermine the aim of his Zen practice in general. This is because, as stated earlier, the fine calligraphic media – the brush and the ink, capture the subtleties of the nervous system of the writer at all times.

A work of traditional Zen calligraphy can thus

never be 'cheated' or forged.

One may experience lucky accidents now and again that look enlightened, of course, but the real test is in one's maintained spontaneity. For can one *always* leave a trace of equanimity no matter when and where one writes?

And the same goes for formal western mindfulness practices. Can we maintain compassion for ourselves and others and remain in the present moment – flowing harmoniously with the wholesome conditions that are already here, no matter what arrives?

It is a tall order, and famously so. Thus, a Zen calligraphy piece begins with ourselves – our habitual relationship to the present moment, and therefore our lifestyle in general, meaning that the brushwork becomes just the tip of the iceberg. For the real work of art is the quality of our hourly, daily, weekly, monthly, yearly cultivation of personal character.

This means that an enlightened Zen master who picks up the brush for the first time will nearly always leave a more wholesome trace than an unenlightened first-timer, because such a master relates to, and thus interacts with, the universe in a more wholesome way.

Therefore, traditional Chinese calligraphy is a fine dance right from the beginning – requiring continually soft, elegant finger movements (which are necessary for 'listening to' and twisting the brush), as well as a lively yet grounded confidence – in order to make energised, vigorous gestures without becoming emotionally aroused.

For when writing Zen calligraphy, ideally there is to be no manic excitement and no frustration – just a sincere pragmatic acceptance of all the necessary conditions of the present moment. Because if the writer does become excited or frustrated, their fluid, fine movements, not to mention their mental calculations, quickly become erratic and clumsy, and their work of calligraphy suffers as a result.

In this regard, the practice of Zen calligraphy is quite similar to tai chi, in fact, and traditional Chinese calligraphy teachers refer to the lively, flowing, fine manipulation of the ink as an expression of 'qi,' even – a smooth, life-affirming energy flow that is healthy for the body and mind.

Thus, if the trace of the qi flow in the calligraphy piece is visibly broken, restricted, or imbalanced (for example, when the tip of the brush is not in the centre of the stroke), it is not considered a good piece of art, because it represents dis-ease – an imbalanced heart, and who wants a trace of that hanging on their living room or office wall?

In this way, traditional Chinese works of art are seen as functional, practical reminders of positive human potential, and Zen calligraphy pieces are judged on their artistic merit according to how thoroughly they satisfy these requirements.

To a western audience, this might sound quite limiting, and yet something similar to the Chinese ideal was proposed by the nineteenth century German philosopher Nietzsche, who was an expert in ancient Greek classical art.

Nietzsche argued, for example – in a similar spirit to that of Zen calligraphers, that art should educate positively as well as entertain – that it should be broadly functional, if it is to enjoy the privilege of being placed on a pedestal in the public domain.

This vision of classical art that spans East and West demands, therefore, that even a traditional calligrapher's choice of words must be in harmony with such an ideal. And yet, despite just a single written Chinese character being acceptable as a work of calligraphy, if its strokes are rendered with a heart polluted by dis-ease, ultimately it does not matter how conceptually profound the use of that particular word is. For the lack of centredness on the part of the author will be discernible in the trace of the brush, and the whole piece will be considered polluted.

Thus, some Japanese Zen calligraphy schools would require new students to write the traditional character for number one – a horizontal line, for a whole year before they could move on to more complicated characters.

This was necessary in order for new disciples to tune in to the mindful handling of the brush, as well as to better understand how succumbing to mental turbulence affects the whole process – rather than become distracted with the easier tasks of memorising the structures of symbols and the general aesthetics of composing finalised pieces.

For just like formal mindfulness meditation, sufficient recognisable progress in Zen calligraphy, and thus true insight into the art, can only arrive after a certain number of dedicated hours have been invested in *physical hard work* (which is the literal Chinese meaning of kung fu (GōngFū – 功夫), in fact).

In this regard, the outcomes of Zen calligraphy

practice, just like yiquan push-hands 'sparring' bouts against competent opponents, give a highly tangible reflection of the efforts that a practitioner has made to transcend their inner chaos – to subdue their ego.

And even though oftentimes they might not like what they feel or see, with repeated mindful exposure to necessary failure, the calligrapher or martial artist can come to more easily accept the 'ugly truths' in his or her life, and suddenly a deeper beauty can appear.

For the artist's intention to continually expand his or her mind and heart – to open up like a flower, in itself leaves an increasingly attractive trace, and not only when laid down via heartful calligraphy strokes, but even as a wholesome social presence – an exuded spiritual 'perfume' to be enjoyed by other people and animals wherever they go.

Thus, the practice of Zen calligraphy 'writes us' to some degree – it forces us into submission to its fine medium. But this truth can easily be surrendered to, because in the opposite direction lies crudeness – unrefined ignorance. And even though ignorance is bliss for periods of time, the counter-truth – that knowledge is power, tends to trump ignorance in the same way that skillful cooperation tends to overcome selfish competitiveness.

Proficient Zen calligraphers, as well as formal mindfulness and Zen meditators, therefore gain a deep conviction in the idea that the most beneficial overall path is that of self-cultivation – a constant refinement, achieved through the relentless pursuit of an improved character, and the positive trace that such an endeavour inevitably leaves in its wake.

6

ZEN CALLIGRAPHY: SURRENDERING

A good Chinese calligraphy brush head tends to have weasel hair at its centre and goat hair surrounding it.

When my calligraphy teacher told me this fact, I burst out laughing, and seeing him laugh just as much at my response, made me laugh even more. For what is so special about a weasel's fur that it is prized by Zen calligraphers? And why complicate matters further by adding goat's hair to the mix?

Well, it transpires that this particular combination of animal hairs is the result of more than three thousand years of Chinese writing system evolution – a process which took into account aesthetic as well as practical philosophical considerations – such as how any trace of one's spirit is left behind on the writing surface.

In the earliest stages of character evolution, however, Chinese pictograms were not rendered with a fine brush. Rather, they were carved into bone with a knife, which caused the resultant strokes to be mostly straight and sharp-tipped.

As time went on, though, written symbols began to be incorporated into bronzeware items, and these symbols' strokes started to undergo changes – they became more rounded, for example, so that when molten metal was poured into their moulded forms, they could be more thoroughly filled.

And after this development had matured, characters began to be written in black ink – on bamboo slats, which were then connected together to form books or scrolls.

It was during this stage, then, that the aesthetics of Chinese characters started to be heavily influenced by the calligraphy brush itself.

What is more, the way that the brush would so easily render fluid organic shapes in a medium that resembled black water caused one talented Daoist philosopher and scholar to intimately connect Chinese calligraphy with the cultivation of the mysterious water-like Dao – both theoretically as well as physically.

And so, the greatest calligrapher in Chinese history, a man called Wáng Xīzhī, literally made his mark – never to be outshone even to this day.

For it is widely agreed that the calligraphy of Wáng

Xīzhī has a noble yet grounded natural presence to it – not unlike a refined Zen meditation posture.

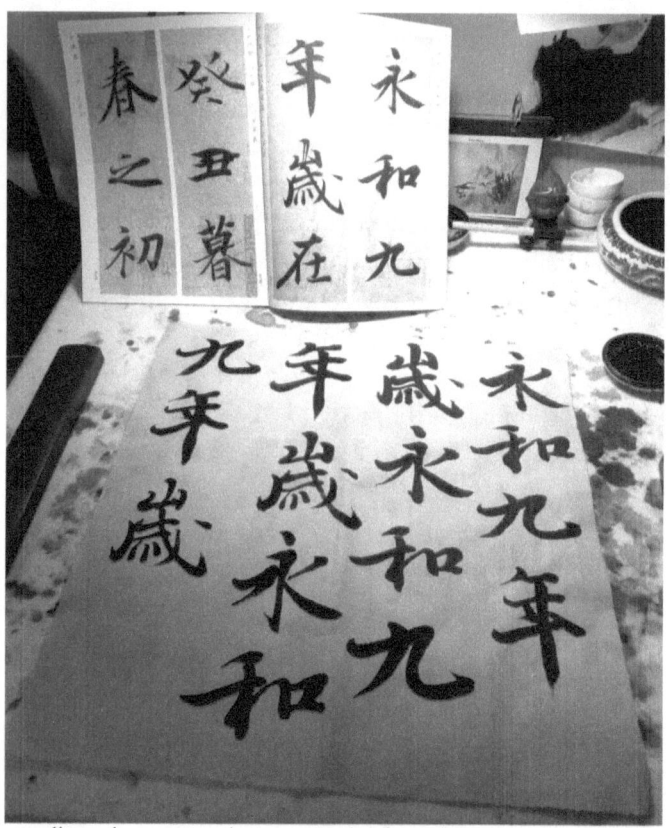

A calligraphy practice sheet written by the author – copying the style of Wáng Xīzhī, in order to tune to the spirit of the ancient Chinese 'Zen' brush.

But how did this master accomplish such a feat, exactly? Well, it can be seen from his written works that he had an appreciation of, and insight into, not only Daoist philosophy, but also such arts as refined swordplay. Thus, it seems that some degree of physical kung fu-style cultivation was incorporated into his calligraphy practice – as a means of flowing more harmoniously with nature when composing his pieces.

For in the same way that a tangible sense of yiquan's springy, lively 'Yì' (意) – the inherent 'cellular intent' possessed by all living systems, was tuned to by ancient kung fu practitioners in order to place their postures, movements, and weapons more in harmony with their true nature, it also apparently directed the construction of the Zen calligraphy brush.

And this meant, therefore, that certain types of animal hair, and combinations thereof, were carefully tested as to how efficiently they allowed the artist to render the trace of lively Yì – universal life-affirming spirit, onto a writing surface.

A good modern calligraphy brush head composed of weasel and goat hair is thus a highly evolved Zen kung fu writing tool – calibrated to deposit a trace of cellular Yì with the least amount of effort on the part of the writer.

As a result, any inherent natural beauty witnessed in the shapes created within a work of traditional Chinese calligraphy may not be so much due to the writer as it is to the clever construction of the brush that he or she used.

For the employment of relatively rigid weasel hair allows for the brush to be imbued with the spirit of the most ancient Chinese calligraphy style – where characters were carved into bones with a knife. And surrounding this more rigid core with softer goat hair enables the more fluid molten metal bronzeware style to also be incorporated – integrated seamlessly, into the brush head body.

What is more, this clever feat of engineering even provides the brush head with a yin-yang quality – a rigid, springy core surrounded by a softer, flowing outer band.

Thus, all a writer who possesses such a tool needs to do is to *allow the Zen brush to express its true nature* – the inherent wisdom that it inherited from the ancient Chinese scholar priests.

And this is where the practice of surrendering to nature in general comes in – of cultivating a harmonious, peaceful heart at all times, so that the profound nature of the cosmos can be harnessed – allowed to do all the 'work.'

This is not the usual situation for professional artists who are seeking personal recognition, however. For why would an artist want to practice writing and selling beautiful calligraphy if they – their ego, cannot take the credit for the outcome?

And yet, an insightful mindfulness practitioner would answer such a question by saying that one practices calligraphy for the same reasons that one sits down to meditate – to cool down, calm down, collect oneself, and so on.

In this respect, a Zen calligraphy piece is more of a by-product of a greater art form – a greater internal practice. And even though at times the judgemental ego inevitably steps in and gets in the way – just like it does during formal mindfulness or Zen meditation, at other times one is too engaged with appreciating the experience of flowing inside the present moment to bother with egotistical concerns.

In amongst all of this, however, one thing is for sure, and that is if one intends to consciously *do* the job of nature – intends to try to actively create beautiful, organic, lively calligraphy strokes, then the outcome will be conflict-driven – dis-eased, and the meditation, as well as any work of art that emerges from it, will be a disaster – just like when one tries to proactively breathe peaceful breaths during formal mindfulness or Zen meditation.

Still, in the world of Zen calligraphy practice, such catastrophe will not always be a *complete* disaster. For even the uncomfortable conditions of feeling one has failed may be worked with – accepted, flowed with and transcended – as an inevitable, natural part of the path, since it is all a *practice*, a journey – a process of unfolding.

Thus, Zen calligraphy, just like formal mindfulness meditation, requires a constant surrendering to the superior power of nature.

And as soon as we can do so with confidence – as soon as we can fully accept that the infinite universe is more powerful than our smaller-minded self, suddenly nature flows through us – it becomes our ally, and we receive its power – an infinite-minded self, and all the necessary loss – *the inevitable pain of being this organic process*, no longer hurts so much, because we have the soothing medicine to treat it – an embodied open acceptance of 'what is.'

But this approach to harnessing nature's power – utilising peaceful acceptance, is nothing new, really, is it? For it has been known to mankind all over the world for thousands, if not tens of thousands, of years.

And yet, *it is always so easily forgotten.*

Thus, a work of Zen calligraphy produced from the act of mindfully surrendering to our nature – with the beauty of humbly accepting 'what is' having been transferred, as the Chinese Daoist proverb goes, 'from heart to hand' (DéXīnYìngShǒu – 得心应手) – from the prosocial mind's positive intention and onto the paper in front of us, serves as a useful reminder of that truth – communicating that we are not ultimately lost souls waiting to be reunited with some greater power.

Rather, we are merely, as well as awesomely, *always a seamless part of this infinitely beautiful universe – we are always 'home,'* and all we need to do is put our feet up, so to speak, and relax deeply – in both body and mind, and allow that truth to manifest all by itself.

However, if we do not have access to a good quality traditional Chinese calligraphy brush to write with – something that is the case for most people on the planet, then our surrendering needs to go a little deeper. For under such circumstances, *we ourselves need to become the brush* – so that we can deliver the pure, unhindered, lively Yì spirit onto the surface in front of us discernibly enough.

This is a more demanding, yet also potentially more liberating, 'kung fu' aspect of Zen calligraphy practice, in fact, which can be manifested by using whatever ink, paint, or painting tool one has to hand – a twig, a feather, or even one's fingers.

And so, in this respect, the Zen calligraphy brush is ultimately more about our own being, rather than something that we need to painstakingly source and purchase.

Thus, when surrendered to and channeled – *made discernible within our own being*, the spirit of a Zen brush may be revealed to the world before it is transferred to a surface in front of us.

For in its most absolute condition, the brush is the cosmic beauty of our organic, upright, robust, yet highly flexible and flowing nature – our lively yet humbled spirit.

7

ZEN CALLIGRAPHY: ANCHORING

A Chinese calligraphy brush is wielded somewhat like a kung fu sword – a Zen blade. And this phenomenon is not a recent development, since the very first Chinese characters were carved into oracle bones with a knife.

Nowadays, though, the metaphorical 'blade' of the brush also incorporates the furnace-hot spirit of the ancient bronzeware style of writing – where the brush head 'melts' the surface that it carves through, leaving behind a durable liquid residue.

Thus, when traditional Chinese calligraphy is written mindfully – as a form of spiritual cultivation, it has a sense of cutting through and melting of illusions about it – as if one were wielding a flaming 'righteous sword.'

And this exact metaphor is represented in traditional Chinese Buddhism via the symbolism associated with a famous bodhisattva called Manjushri – a saintly warrior figure, who sits in an upright meditation posture whilst holding a sword that resembles a flame – a symbolic representation of the energy of our refined mind as it cleaves through the propaganda of the ego.

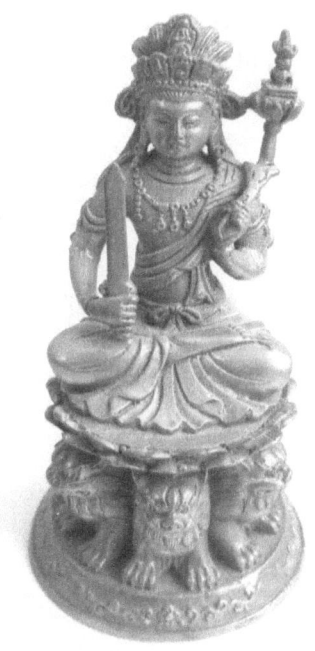

A bronze statue of Manjushri – the 'Bodhisattva of Wisdom.'

So whether we are aware of it or not, by intending to hold our minds upright as we sit in formal mindfulness or Zen meditation, we 'wield' Manjushri's sword.

For once our mind-sword's edge has become fine enough, we can then relax into its sharpness – an increased clarity of perception, and allow the ego's crude foot soldiers to simply march onto our fine posture – to be automatically sliced into pieces.

Of course, this is all a metaphor – perhaps grim, and yet life can be grim at times, since we can feel 'lost at sea' – battered and disorientated by crashing waves and gales, which causes us to seek a strong, tangible sense of *anchor* – if we know where to look, that is.

In western secular mindfulness meditation, this anchor is most often found in aspects of our breathing – via the friction caused by the air entering our nostrils, as well as the friction that can be felt between bodily tissues at the top of the belly just below the diaphragm – as our chest cavity expands and contracts.

When writing Zen calligraphy, however, our anchor becomes the friction between the blade-like brush and the writing surface. And that very act of seeking to maintain a constant sense of friction as one fluidly manipulates the fine brush 'demands' that one's body and mind assume the same conditions as are present during formal seated mindfulness meditation, in fact.

For if, when writing Zen calligraphy, one does not seek congruence with one's fluid, truth-seeking heart – something that requires a full surrender to the lively cutting and searing nature of the brush, one will inevitably fail in one's objective to leave a wholesome trace on the paper.

Unsurprisingly, perhaps, the same logic applies when wielding a good tai chi sword effectively, since one must surrender to the noble spiritual insight of the Zen sword-maker – how the fine weapon cleaves the air as a result of his or her practical insights, for example. For in doing so, one *inherits those insights.*

In Zen calligraphy, therefore, a sense of cutting – of penetrating friction, is essential to the art. And even when the brush leaves the paper and 'leaps into the air,' the feeling of grounded friction is still followed as a trace left within the body, since after many hours of diligent, mindful practice, eventually this feeling becomes established in one's nervous system in a familiar way – as an aptitude, that traditional Chinese calligraphers call a 'sense of brush.'

With the brush head digging into the paper, then – like a dragon's claw sharpening itself on the tough 'fabric' of nature, one skilfully 'carves' with ink – searing one's chosen characters with one's life energy – with qi, which allows one's muscles and circulatory system to enjoy an exhilarating expansion – a wholesome calisthenic catharsis.

For unlike western calligraphy, this process is not one of intending to perfectly replicate a prescribed outward form with rigid, robot-like control. Rather, it is one of intending to perform a perfect inner balancing act in precisely the same manner as when practicing formal mindfulness meditation – by maintaining an expansive, fluid, noble centredness that gives rise to a graceful poise, and thus the ability to make any necessary fine adjustments swiftly, spontaneously, and smoothly.

When writing Zen calligraphy, one therefore conserves one's sense of friction – of anchor, whilst engaging practically – skillfully, with the constant change that is arriving within and without.

And such a feat is achieved via a conscious balancing of all natural conditions that are within one's power to control (or to relinquish control of), so that one can remain upright and functional, even whilst potentially being buffeted by the prevailing winds of the judgmental mind.

In fact, this dynamic uprightness becomes the tangible, inspirational value of the discipline – discernible within the ever-changing, yet aesthetically-balanced structures of the characters one writes – as a focused, wholesome, single-minded flow, an outpouring of Zen cultivation – a journey through the landscape of noble ideals.

When viewing works of Zen calligraphy, therefore, we may momentarily 'borrow' the anchor of the writer – by firstly getting to know the Way of Chinese calligraphy, and then stepping into the artist's shoes as we move along through the piece – from where the brush started, to where it finished – as if writing the work ourselves, and feeling the positive condition of heart that it is communicating.

In this way, such works of fine art – of fine skill, can easily become a kind of invaluable social resource, and especially so when they are embedded within one's culture as a familiar phenomenon.

Thus, everywhere one goes in China, one finds

works of traditional Chinese calligraphy – in temples and teahouses, for example, and in any other places people visit to seek refuge from the inevitable storms that rage all around and within us.

Instead of being at the mercy of any such storm's brutal energies, then, we may skilfully surf and dance upon its surface – becoming more like playful, frolicking dragons, flowing in harmony with our sense of dynamic qi, our claws digging deep into the mysterious flowing Dao, as we follow the Way of Zen calligraphy – anchored in nature's innate wisdom.

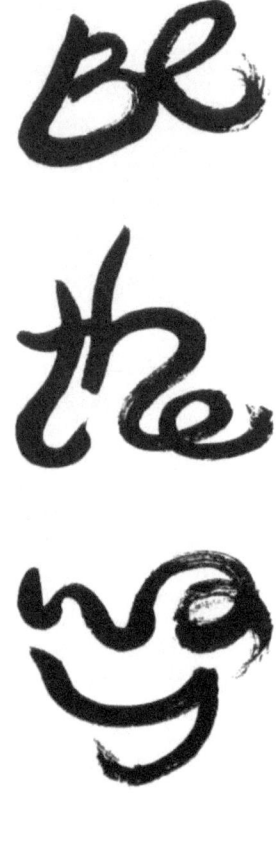

A zen calligraphy piece, which reads, 'Be the Way.'
Written in English by the author.

8

ZEN INK PAINTING: NATURE

It is a well-known fact that spending time in nature – such as when gardening, walking in a park, or wandering through beautiful mountain scenery, is incredibly beneficial for our overall sense of wellbeing. But what if we cannot leave our desks and meeting rooms in order to go out to the countryside as often as we would like to?

One solution would be to buy some houseplants, perhaps. And yet, it is normally out of the question to bring any other aspects of natural scenery – hills, rivers, lakes, forests, and wildlife, into our work and living spaces.

In the offices of medieval China, however, there

were often lots of papers, inks, and good calligraphy brushes at workers' disposal. And so, as officers spent their days tied to their desks, they began, with great enthusiasm and joy, to paint the natural sceneries within which they wished to refresh themselves.

In fact, modern studies have shown that just looking at pictures of nature can benefit us quite considerably. Thus, many medieval Chinese scholars transcended their vocational restrictions by painting scenes of natural phenomena – of people, animals, plants and landscapes, that could help them to relax into a more organic and wholesome frame of mind.

And yet, since these literati were not professional artists with time and energy to devote to producing photorealistic representations of what they saw in their minds' eyes, they instead used their 'kung fu' skills – their Zen calligraphy abilities that they had honed as part of their standard education, in order to achieve their artistic goals.

In this respect, the Chinese scholars utilised the more graphical aspects of traditional Chinese Zen calligraphy to *write* the forms of their desired objects into their paintings – in order to create simple images that broke free from the standard pictographic forms used in Chinese writing.

And as time went on, this practice gained widespread popularity – with adherents realising that many of the restrictions that applied to works of calligraphy need not apply to calligraphy-style 'written paintings.'

However, in order to maintain the organic liveliness and a sense of functionally flowing 'qi' that

Zen Ink Painting

was common to both works of Zen calligraphy and the organic natural world, they sought to preserve the trace of the flowing Zen brush within their depictions.

For what these scholars valued most in nature was the life-affirming, lively 'Yì' (意) – the natural cellular intent, wherever it could be found, and the Zen calligraphy brush had the spirit of Yì built into it.

Thus, the main objective of the medieval Zen ink painters became to render visible – tangible, the Yì of the natural objects that they wished to be closer to. And they would accomplish such a goal with some help from the hairs of their calligraphy brush.

This was a simple enough solution to the predicament of being office-bound whilst also thirsty for natural experiences, and yet it was also an innovation that went on to create a whole new painting tradition – namely, black and white Zen ink painting, or written natural intent painting (XiěYìGuóHuà – 写意国画).

And at this point, perhaps one may begin to identify a discernible pattern with regards to the Chinese names of these traditional Zen arts – particularly so within the names of yiquan kung fu and xieyi painting, for example. For both of these arts' names emphasise the necessary sourcing and utilising of lively natural 'Yì' for the benefit of both mind and body.

However, such an approach was not apparently unique to China, even, since the ancient Greeks had a concept that was very similar to what the Chinese called 'Yì.'

It seems that it has taken until the discovery of the

scientific theory of autopoiesis, though, and the clinical validation of secular mindfulness, for inherent natural intention, or essential biological drive, to be rediscovered as a widely appreciated and potent concept in the West.

For more contemporary western philosophers did refer to, and still continue to contemplate, something akin to this inherent natural drive – apparently calling it *conatus*. But for some reason it has been defined as something slightly different by each philosopher who has approached the topic.

Modern secular mindfulness philosophy, on the other hand, seeks to engage with that very tangible domain of being that lies beyond thoughts – beyond personal definitions, towards a direct immersion in the territory of pure physical nature. For when one is within that 'naturescape,' then the natural intention of objects is pretty clear – trees grow towards sunlight, clouds swirl and billow, water flows downwards, and mountains just sit there with majestic dignity.

Nevertheless, when practicing mindfulness meditation, the idea that one must 'just let go' into this nature can be quite a daunting one. Because what is this alleged 'safety net' of nature doing or arising from, exactly? *What supportive intelligence, if any, is there waiting to catch us on 'the other side' when we take our leap of faith?*

Zen arts' answer is that one leaps towards, or lets go into, one's inherent sophistication – one's reflexively prosocial autopoiesis, or what Chinese Buddhists have called 'Buddha Nature.'

For our healthy *instinctively communal* cells that

manifest automatically and directly from our basic chemical drive *are always on our side* – and famously so, if one takes Richard Dawkins' book, *The Selfish Gene,* as logical and correct.

Thus, feelings and representations of life-affirming positive natural intent that arrive to us from beyond the domain of thoughts – when practicing seated meditation, or watching a ballet dancer or a tai chi master perform, or when viewing Zen calligraphy, reading Zen poetry, listening to spiritual music, and so on, can become wholesome medicine for our civil hearts when we are suffering the colder, sharper aspects of our existence.

And the potential therapeutic value offered by a black and white traditional Chinese Zen ink painting is no different.

For when engaged with by a viewer, such a work of fine art draws attention to the energising, lively springy cellular qualities inherent within natural objects, which can nourish and invigorate our spirits – akin, perhaps, to drinking a cup of freshly brewed green tea.

What Zen calligraphy does with rendered words, then, Zen ink painting accomplishes with universally recognisable natural forms, which have more potential to put the artist's subject matter across to a viewer than does calligraphy.

Thus, Zen ink paintings have a wider conceivable global audience than calligraphy pieces do. And yet, a painting's deeper message can be a lot more ambiguous than a calligraphed statement.

Ultimately, though, just like for Zen calligraphy

pieces, the most important property or communicated 'message' for Zen ink paintings is the trace of the fine, springy brush being laid down onto the paper with a sense of sincere surrender.

This being so, there is much more scope within ink paintings for variety in strokes and ink shade, of course, than there is for traditional Chinese calligraphy – which tends to give Zen ink paintings a more busy or layered appearance.

For the aesthetic objective in the Zen 'written painting' tradition is not to render an abstract calligraphic symbol composed of black dots and lines, but rather to use such simple shapes and strokes to render natural forms of varying shade and texture in the most direct and efficient way.

As a result, the manipulation of watered-down ink and a variety of textures – produced by laying the brush down on its side, using half-dried ink, or moving the brush quickly to create a streaked 'flying white' (FēiBái – 飞白) effect, may be employed to more efficiently and effectively depict certain qualities of the objects being painted – and ideally without losing the trace of the lively brush hairs.

The task of painting Zen-affirming nature is therefore more complex than writing Zen calligraphy. However, unlike the various characters of a calligraphy piece, the forms being rendered in an ink painting have no rigid compositional placement or chronological order of appearance.

Thus, once a competent sense of tone and framed composition – *of ink shade and empty space*, has been gained by a Zen ink painter, the cognitive strain of producing a final piece is not that different from writing calligraphy – allowing a painter to maintain the mindful meditative component easily enough.

For all the painter needs to do is lend their energy and vision to the springy brush hairs – so that the fibres can express their inherent liveliness without the restraining factor of the painter's ego-driven desires.

The process of Zen painting or calligraphy – of leaving a trace of Zen brush, can take care of itself, then, if we allow it to – just like our reflexive breathing can.

And so, a successfully performed Zen ink painting therefore belongs more to nature, the lively Yì – the dynamic ever-present intent of the spacious ever-changing universe, as well as, of course, to the brush, than to any human ego – just like a Zen calligraphy piece does.

In fact, due to this relatively impersonal dimension to Zen ink painting practice, many medieval Zen artists did not even sign their work, since they did not want to encourage the toxicity of their ego to interfere with their peaceful joy – their spiritual freedom, that arose as they engaged with the profoundly soothing sensations of flowing ink and brush.

In this light, the realism of a Zen ink painting's composition and structural elements thus need not be of too much concern.

And yet, there are boundaries that can be crossed, of course – meaning that over time, as practitioners experimented and tried different ways to spontaneously and effectively express the natural spirits of trees, mountains, bamboo, flowers, and so forth, certain standard forms and techniques appeared that satisfied the painters' requirements in an optimal way.

As a result, Zen ink paintings tend to have certain recognisable core motifs and textures that all practitioners within the tradition like to master and replicate.

For ultimately these paintings are not created in order to celebrate originality or personal identity per se, but rather to celebrate nature's universal inherent potential to support and nourish us – as well as our own potential to befriend the wilderness through an impersonal, transcendent appreciation of the inherent affinities that exist between natural objects and our human condition.

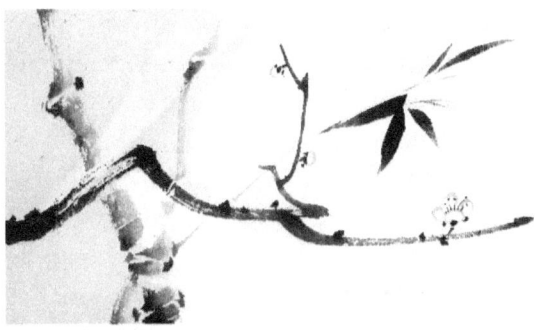

A classical style Chinese zen painting of bamboo and a plum blossom, which uses clear calligraphy style strokes. Created by the author.

And it is also for this precise reason (perhaps unsurprisingly by now), that we sit down to practice formal mindfulness meditation – to borrow the dignity of a mountain, for example, and allow tension to flow down and out of our bodies as if it is being carried away by streams and rivers – in order for us to relax, expand, and open like a flower, with our attention riding the waves of the breath like a leaf on the surface of water.

Therefore, as we paint a Zen ink painting, we also meditate mindfully – we tune to and follow our sense of wholesome natural intent that is always present somewhere in the space within and around us.

This is so that we may better relax into our organic momentum, which in turn enables us to more effortlessly render that natural intent when depicting life-affirming, energetic natural forms.

Ideally, this results in the viewer, who is first and foremost the painter, relaxing further into his or her true nature – giving rise to a continuous feedback cycle that can bring about a deeply wholesome flow.

And such a practice may even produce highly abstract compositions at times – content that is quite abstruse when it comes to its recognisable forms.

For just a few simple strokes can be enough to communicate momentary inspiration – to preserve a direct trace, or a visible record, of, for example, infinite space dappled with cosmic energy – a positive, life-affirming, invigorating natural potency that is always surrounding and penetrating us – in varying shades, textures, and dynamic organic spirit.

9

ZEN INK PAINTING: ASYMMETRY

There is a creative exercise that some Japanese Zen monks like to practice, which requires painting dots along a strip of paper at randomly spaced intervals.

It may sound like a pretty simple activity, and yet people who try it quickly realise that it is a lot more difficult to accomplish than they had imagined.

For in their attempts to replicate the randomness that is discernible in the natural world, they discover that their minds' inclinations towards creating order continually get in the way of their efforts.

Nevertheless, meditators and artists alike can derive great value from undertaking such an exercise, since it can help them to remain aware of how they might become their own worst enemies – how their inclinations towards controlling the natural asymmetry of the cosmos can upset their efforts to exist in harmony with nature.

For unless we wish to suffer every unpredictable yet inevitable misfortune with a scowl and a clenched fist, and thus grow increasingly unhinged over time, we must feel at ease with randomness – with the weather from one day to the next, for example, as well as the arbitrary loss of loved ones and aspects of our health.

Therefore, no matter whether through formal seated mindfulness or Zen meditation, yoga, tai chi, Zen calligraphy, Zen ink painting, and so on, finding ways to practice maintaining an internal balance in amongst unavoidable external chaos – amongst all the cosmic natural imbalances, is apparently crucial to sustaining our day-to-day functionality.

It is arguable, even, that the above-mentioned dot writing exercise lies at the heart of traditional Chinese Zen ink painting, because the 'imperfection' of such randomness – *the inherent unfairness of the universe*, is in fact what makes our universe *naturally functional*.

For without the chaotic friction of the cosmos, there would be no muddy 'womb' created at the bottom of a pond, for example – no nutrient-rich, dank, dark, water-logged matrix that enables a lotus seed to sprout and blossom into a beautiful flower.

Confidently being or playing host to any of this natural 'imperfection' is incredibly difficult, though, and especially so when the perception of an inherently unfair universe is so easily labelled as a faulted perception – an image to be replaced, however

Zen Ink Painting

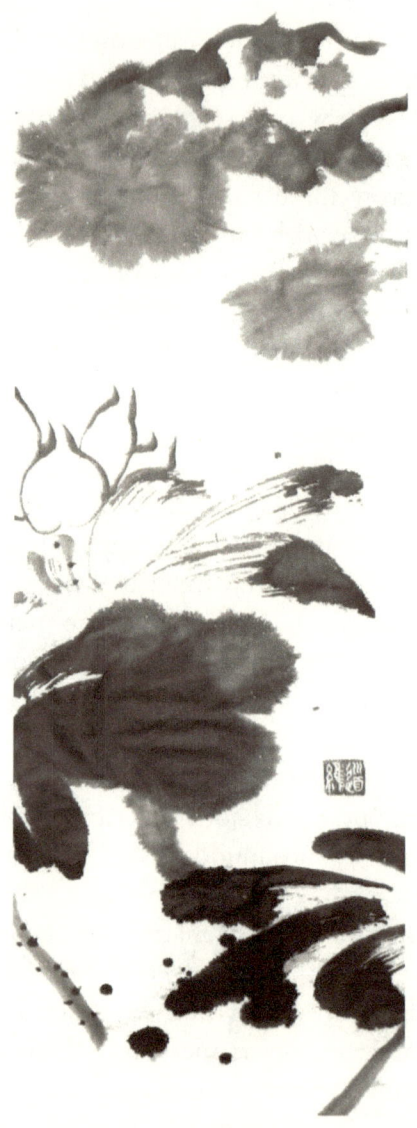

A zen painting of lotus plants, created by the author after ink was randomly splashed onto the paper.

irrationally, with an imagined much fairer universe that operates 'just fine' in our mind's eye.

Such a perfectly imagined universe would perhaps be full of lollipop trees spaced equidistantly on an equilateral triangle mountain slope. But how does this fairer universe allow for the trees on the southern and northern slopes, let alone the farmers growing vegetables on those respective inclines, to naturally receive the same amount of sunshine? For as we know, the southern slopes tend to be favoured more by plants due to the greater amounts of sunlight that they receive there.

Suddenly, our imagined fairer, purer, more balanced, symmetrical universe is no longer as simple and 'equal' as we thought, and we need to wake up – to 'get real.' And this is where acceptance of 'what is' can begin – with letting go of the apparent perfection of an imagined existential symmetry, so that we may embrace *the more functional perfection of the real organic asymmetry within and around us.*

This exact sentiment is utilised by formal mindfulness practitioners, even – when they ride their 'analog' reflexive breathing in favour of indulging their 'digital' thoughts, for example. For the practical truth – the domain within which we live and die, lies not in what we mathematically plan or wish – not in what we merely *think* should be, but instead in the raw economic reality of *'what is.'*

Thus, as the Chinese ancient art of fengshui reminds us, the southern slopes are always more favourable than the northern ones. And so, instead of wishing that the natural universe was otherwise constructed (which only creates a depressed state of mind), one can heartily accept the inherent asymmetry of nature, and expand one's intelligent potential so that one may thrive more comfortably.

And this insight was well-appreciated by the medieval Chinese Zen painters, who set asymmetry as a fundamental 'rule' for their compositions – observed by the painter paying careful attention to the sizes, groupings, and spacings of visual elements, as well as the overall 'weighting' of the image as a whole.

This was not just to make the distribution of elements look more visually realistic – more natural, it also gave the overall piece a sense of being in dynamic existential harmony with the inherently asymmetrical practical universe all around and within it.

A competently rendered Zen ink painting will therefore always have a composition that distributes ink-filled parts and empty parts in a way that gives the whole image a sense of yin and yang harmoniously and dynamically interplaying with one another.

Thus, whiter 'blanket' elements, such as clouds, sky, and sparkling water, are often used to open up vast empty 'yin' spaces, allowing for *an abstract yet tangible dynamic symmetry* – a sense of organically distributed yet balanced flowing qi, to be maintained throughout.

For if we consider, for a moment, how we manage our daily lives – by balancing work and rest, foraging and consumption, speaking and listening, giving and receiving, and so forth, all of this does indeed take place in an asymmetrical universe – where there is an arrow of time causing objects to constantly wear down to the point of dysfunction.

Asymmetry

A traditional Zen ink painting's composition is therefore simply a visual representation of this situation, in order that the viewer may be inspired to move through their naturally asymmetrical lives in a more practical way – more aware of nature's inherent organic beauty, and thus more accepting of impurity and inevitable dysfunction in general.

Because even though when facing a 'yin-yang' symbol it can seem quite obvious that our constant internal energy balancing occurs amidst dynamic conditions that are asymmetrical, it is rather difficult to remain mindful of it as one moves away into the more stimulating, complex, and often symmetrically-organised social environments that we must spend most of our time within.

In this light, then, Chinese people found ways to place the more asymmetrical motifs present within Zen ink paintings not only on their walls, but on clothing, crockery, external architecture, within the layout of their gardens, and so on – giving rise to a unique and very particular cultural aesthetic.

And this Zen-driven difference between Chinese and western culture can be witnessed rather vividly when, for example, one compares images of the royal gardens of Tang and Song Dynasty Chinese emperors to their nearest equivalents in Europe.

For the traditional European royal gardeners most often aspired towards imposing digitally perfect mathematical reflectional symmetries onto their environments, whilst their Chinese counterparts, on the other hand, sought harmony with the natural asymmetry that originated from the heavens and the earth.

In this way, China's relatively early 'mindfulness revolution,' which championed the acceptance of asymmetry in the name of practical functionality, is vividly apparent as a deeply-embedded cultural phenomenon. And it remains in use today, even – via asymmetrical structural and organisational elements installed within newly built Chinese parks, universities, schools, tourist attractions, and so forth.

It seems that the West has only quite recently begun waking up to the wisdom inherent in the concept of embracing asymmetric balance, therefore. And yet, as time goes on, with the East continuing to appropriate western 'developed world' values as it grows more powerful – something that will require these two cultural extremes to interact and interweave on a more intensive basis, perhaps there will be lively ongoing reciprocal change in the West also – a cultural evolution that moves towards a more zen-oriented perspective.

In any case, this is already happening within present-day western secular mindfulness communities. For when mindfulness students hope to reach their ideals of practice, but fail, a grounded respect for the awkward asymmetry inherent in their efforts-to-progress expectations is often encouraged. This is achieved by practitioners being urged to see 'full catastrophes' as inevitable life events, for example – via a reframing of any impeding, self-defeating ignorance or random misfortune as being an integral, necessary part of the path to greater success.

As a result, there is now the oft-spoken adage that

one 'fails one's way to success' – through trial and error, which is a practice that lies at the heart of the scientific method, even.

For to lose one's balance – to trip over and fall, is not automatically an error. It is, rather, merely a product of operating within a universe where not every obstacle can be predicted or identified early enough in order to be skilfully negotiated.

In other words, to meet a setback is the natural result of attempting to proactively attain one's ideals in the face of inevitable adversity – meaning that one need not admit defeat at the first sign of inconvenience. Rather, one can continue marching forward – so that there can be at least *some* hope of arriving at the proverbial mountain-top.

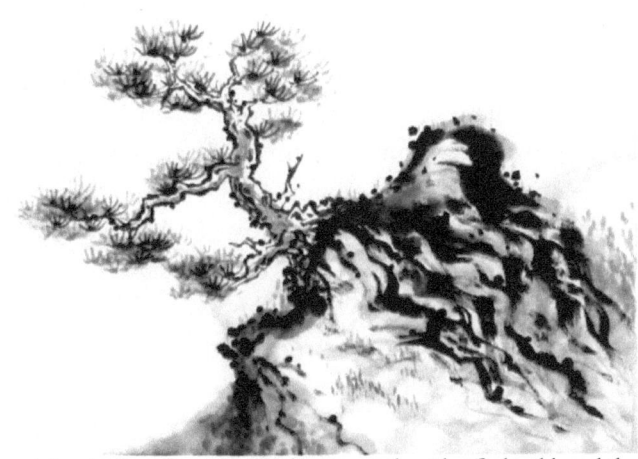

A zen ink painting of a pine tree clinging to the side of a boulder whilst reaching up to the sky. Created by the author.

Thus, a comfort with the inherent awkwardness of our practical existential situation is represented by a Zen ink painting of, for example, a weather-beaten, stunted, gnarled pine tree clinging to the side of a cliff – its branches and lush needles vibrant with vigorous intent, reaching up to the heavens no matter its predicament.

For many of us can feel that we are, or have been, weathering similar conditions to that pine tree, and so the tree's emphasised relentless intent – to keep pushing onwards and upwards no matter what, becomes deeply symbolic to us.

Such a practical mode of being, and the organic asymmetry that it is so entwined with, can even cause mindfulness meditators *to actively seek out and indulge in nature's inherent asymmetry whenever possible* – to proactively invite into their lives the inherent beauty that accompanies random chaos – as the artist Jackson Pollock did with his 'drip painting' artworks, for example – albeit in a disciplined manner.

As far as painting in a relatively random way goes, however, such a 'welcoming chaos' approach is far from novel for Chinese people. For more than one thousand years ago, during the Tang Dynasty, the Chinese painter WángMò (王墨) promoted his 'splashed ink' (PōMò – 泼墨) landscape painting method – the spirit of which was eventually taken up, and further built upon, by Zen monks in Japan.

For the ultimate goal of such a practice was to render the true nature of our organic yet sophisticated existence in as simple and direct a manner as possible – by embedding tangibly positive, lively, inspiring

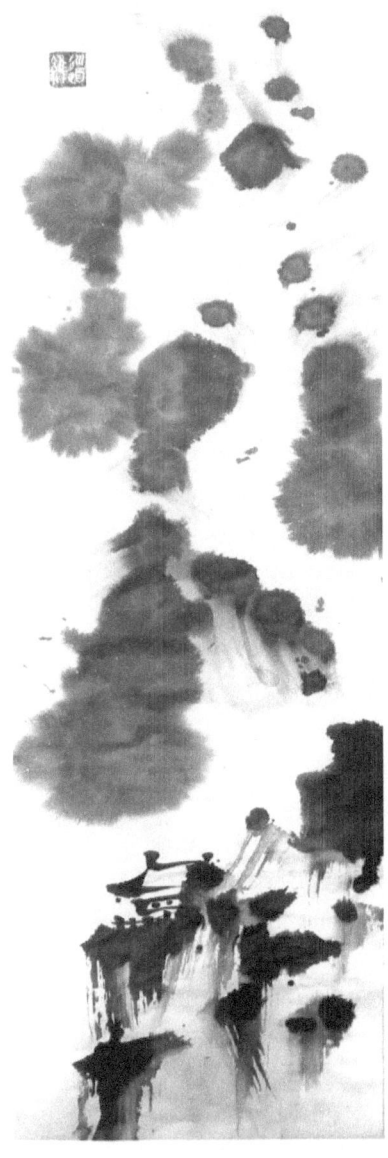

A PōMò style zen ink painting of a mountain scene, created by the author.

forms within chaotic surroundings.

In Japan, this is known as 'wabi sabi' aesthetics, and in the West it may be called 'a diamond in the rough.'

Thus, medieval Zen painters would seek to manage chaotic splashes of 'drunken ink' in various ways – with their fingers, even, and with skillful calligraphy strokes, in order to frame and *dynamically balance* any asymmetrical patterns that had appeared – so that the ever-present catastrophic dimension of the universe could be transformed into something more wholesome.

This painting practice was a kind of meditation in itself, therefore, just like when mindfulness meditators practice reframing chaotic thoughts as mere random 'rumours' – as echoes of bygone cultural voices, and then return their attentions to the wholesome sensations of their breathing – the outcome of which is an increase in their general resilience.

For to constantly attempt to find an adequate internal balance in amongst the natural chaos of the universe keeps our 'acceptance muscles' toned and tested – as we skilfully adapt and adjust our mental and physical structures in order to remain upright and centred – so that we may come to *appreciate natural, inevitable chaos*, even.

And some Japanese Zen practitioners took this sentiment as far as actively smashing their finely made teacups, creating unique asymmetrical fractures throughout each vessel's structure – as an appreciable imprint of chaotic nature.

This pattern would then be preserved and emphasised by repairing the cup with a silver or gold lacquer – causing it to appear more naturally beautiful than before.

Such Zen-inspired repairing of cups and bowls, called *kintsugi*, and the resultant natural beauty that it renders, has already become a powerful metaphor used in secular mindfulness circles, in fact. This is because it highlights how accidents and flaws can improve an object or person – perhaps along the lines of the philosopher Nietzsche's famous statement, 'what does not kill us makes us stronger.'

For an asymmetry between individuals – of wealth, climate, physical aesthetics, education, strength, health, testosterone, oestrogen, and so forth, is an unavoidable truth in all of our societies. And so, the more that we accept it and flow with it when it is inevitable, the more in harmony with the natural universe we will be, and the more empowered we will become as a result – by way of being able to turn what seem to be weaknesses into strengths.

In this light, then, the celebration of asymmetry in Zen ink paintings is indeed a very practical and intelligent inclusion. Because we are so often engaged in analysing and balancing our various daily and weekly activities with a mathematical engineering mindset, that the assumed digital 'perfection' of such a mentality overflows into and colours our vision of how a functional natural universe should be constructed – most often as perfectly symmetrical in all ways, which is a mindset that the Vietnamese Zen master Thich Nhat Hanh has called an 'equality complex.'

For from such an equality-heavy perspective, any differences between genders, religions, national ideologies, and so on, just cannot be fully accepted. And it is this fundamental non-acceptance, rooted in obsessive mathematical thinking, that makes us more dysfunctional as humans, since we cannot tolerate unavoidable natural asymmetry when it does appear.

In the interest of a healthier outlook, therefore, we must recognise that entertaining aspirations towards perfect equivalencies within our cosmos – between social philosophies, ethnicities, sexualities, and so forth, will only lead to greater social dysfunction.

Zen ink paintings thus seek to disencumber such inherent imbalances – with a presentation on the beauty of imbalance itself, so that we may accept our misfortunes and mistakes, and move on to something more practical – *more internally balanced*, regarding the truth of our inherently asymmetrical natural world. For where there is a yang, *there is always a complementary yin*, and vice versa – *if we have the momentary insight to identify it.*

In this regard, then, Zen ink paintings highlight the imperfection inherent in imagined perfection – via an internally balanced celebration of the essential asymmetry of natural form and function – of 'what is.'

People who appreciate Zen ink paintings' profound asymmetry may therefore maintain a better sense of functional dynamic balance as they move through their daily lives – as they allow the random arrival of unavoidable chaotic, naturally 'perfect' events to take their necessary course – beyond any need for conscious control.

10

ZEN INK PAINTING: MOUNTAINS

When a traditional Zen gardener plans a new landscaping project, they firstly map out how they will arrange the biggest stones. Then they pay careful attention to how water will arrive on and around that landscape – envisioning where any plants will take root.

In this respect, the larger stones of a garden represent its compositional 'bones,' or 'mountains' – structures that govern where and how moisture, and thus life, will flow through that space.

And it is not only the structures of gardens that are governed in this way, for all natural landscapes are heavily influenced by the interactions between mountains and waters – the two main antagonistic geological 'forces.'

This is not a new idea, though – it has been appreciated by cultures all over the world, and was particularly strong in ancient China, where a distinctive kind of painting that celebrated the natural law of the high and the low, the rising and falling, as well as the rigid and flowing elements of our environment became very popular.

These works were given their own genre, even – namely, 'mountain and water paintings' (ShānShuǐGuóHuà). And it seems that after having been transported to the West as cultural curiosities, such imagery inspired the beginning of what we now call the western landscape painting tradition.

It also predated the appearance of Zen gardens in China, as well as Chinese Zen ink paintings, resulting in both of those traditions being able to absorb into their repertoires much of the aesthetics associated with the already fashionable penchant for depicting mountains and water together.

What is more, the competent rendering of various mountain textures in ink became a benchmark for the level of brush skill of a Zen ink painter.

For out of all the traditional elements that can populate a Zen ink painting, stones and mountains are the most 'dead' when it comes to the life-affirming natural intent that the painter intends to imbue their forms with.

Thus, finely-rendered mountains are considered the greatest challenge for the Zen ink painter, since the artist needs to have, in addition to competent skill in

Zen Ink Painting

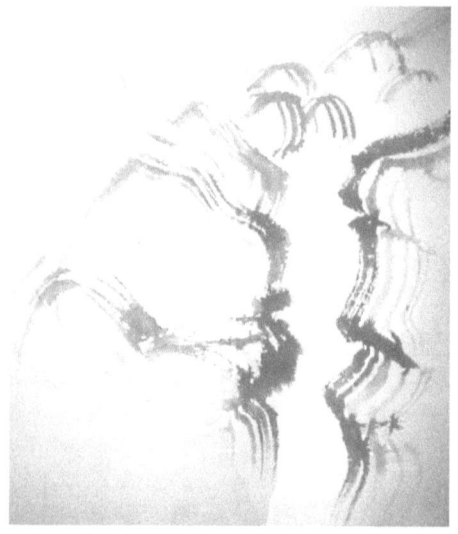

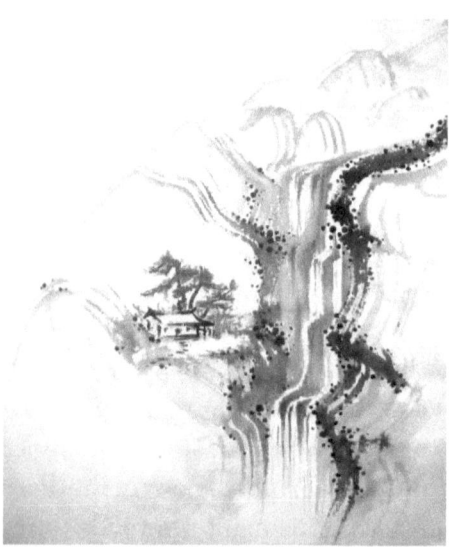

A misty mountain waterfall zen ink painting shown in two stages of completion. Created by the author.

using a brush, ink, and compositional theory, a good enough understanding of a mountain's true 'spirit,' so that even an object made of cold hard stone can be depicted in a wholesome manner – can be 'brought to life,' so to speak.

It is here, then, with respect to this particular challenge of painting mountains, where formal seated mindfulness and Zen meditation can step into the picture, since these disciplines are often described as 'sitting like a mountain' – elevated, with the noble, majestic dignity of a grounded prominence.

For once the Zen ink painter has practiced meditating like a mountain, and has therefore gained any insight into the connection between the human condition and these magnificently elevated objects, his or her experience can then be used to influence the aesthetics of a mountain and water painting.

For example, the painter can be more enlightened as to where a 'meditative' mountain should be placed in a composition, and how to form its general shape.

Furthermore, by embodying the grounded, peaceful dignity of a mountain, the painter can feel more anchored within his or her being as they surrender to the inherently life-affirming nature of the Zen brush.

Because no matter the season that arrives – summer, with its blistering heat, or winter, with its icy frosts, a mountain just sits through it all – unmoved, with dignified acceptance.

And such a regal essence or quality particular to mountains can be emphasised within a Zen ink painting by adorning steep slopes with crowns or cloaks of vegetation, or by embellishing a prominence's virtuous uprightness with plummeting waterfalls.

One may even decorate its majestic inclines with gem-like boulders – nestled within nooks or piled at its feet, and accentuate its resilient diamond-like spirit by outlining various crystalline facets – using contour lines, rough textures, and varying shades of light ink to render an uncut natural appearance – as if the elevation were a giant organic jewel pressed firmly into the earth.

The surface of a mountain can then be polished and softened by the flow of clouds and water over and around its impressive form – guiding pilgrims to its feet, so that they may prostrate themselves and bathe in its aura, as many Tibetan Buddhists do at the foot of Mount Kailash today.

When creating a Zen landscape, then, one is, in a sense, attempting to know the creative heart of nature itself – attempting to 'meet one's creator,' whilst remaining as alive as possible, of course.

This is so that one's depictions of powerful, natural forms – such as mountains, oceans, rivers, clouds, and so on, may be imbued with wholesome, resilient, vigorous spirit, and can also be arranged within the composition in a functional manner – so that a sense of potent organic harmony can arise between them.

And this notion that harmonious interaction between mountains and water is the origin of all of life's essential qualities is prominent, even, in ancient Indian spiritual stories – with the most famous theme being that of a mountain that can churn the milky ocean of the cosmos – creating numerous powerful objects in the process, including an elixir of immortality.

For mountains reach upwards and point to the extremes of the heavens, whilst water flows downwards with irrepressible enthusiasm – into the potent life-incubating earth. And this symbolism harks back to Confucius' teachings in *The Analects* (Chapter 6 (Yōng Yě – 雍也), Verse 23), in fact – where he emphasises that mountains, in being tranquil and long-lived, are enjoyed by the virtuous, whilst water, in being active and spritely, is enjoyed by the wise (ZhìZhěYàoShuǐRénZhěYàoShān – 知者乐水仁者乐山).

Thus, in a sense, traditional Chinese mountain and water paintings represent inner psychological landscapes linked to the enthusiastic cultivation of the Confucian view of the human heart.

When it comes to the features of more definitively 'Zen' landscape paintings, however, qualities experienced during formal Zen (or mindfulness 'spacious awareness') meditation – where the practitioner openly senses raw 'analog data' within infinite spaciousness, tends to be the focus – represented via myriad layers of peaks, mists, and river valleys, for example, as they peter out towards the distant horizon.

Zen mountains and water can thus be considered as akin to two abstract dual fundamental forces of nature – like yin and yang, or the heavens and the earth – two primary spiritual elements that can represent our existential extremes, and thus the fundamental concepts that influence how we view and understand our cosmos.

And as it happens, a famous Chinese Zen teaching involving mountains, water, and the path to enlightenment, points to this very idea, even.

For a Tang Dynasty Chinese Zen master, called Qīngyuán Wéixìn (青原惟信), stated that at first one sees mountains are absolutely mountains, and waters are absolutely waters. Then, as one enters the Zen path and gains more insight into the constantly changing truth of nature, one recognises that such labels as 'mountains' and 'waters' are rather arbitrarily awarded, since their reality depends on one's practical situation.

For example, mountains can flow downwards like water, and waves can rise up like mountains. Therefore, one may practice transcending such awkward permanent labels as 'mountains' and 'waters' until one finally gains enlightenment – an event that requires a full acceptance of the necessary impermanence of all objects, including one's concept of a self.

And once this has been achieved, Qīngyuán Wéixìn stated that mountains once again become the mountains they were before, and the same goes for waters – because one fully accepts that each labelled form has its own relative truth, and thus potential value, no matter all forms' absolute emptiness of any permanent identity.

The mountains of Zen ink landscape painting are therefore not always just places the painter would like to hike up into or around – they tend to serve much deeper purposes.

They may encourage the viewer to transcend the

concept-driven mind that attaches to absolutes, for example, or to conquer the emotion-driven concerns of the ego by befriending the unavoidable mountain-like obstacles in life – to climb their seemingly infinitely-high cliffs in an intimate and humble fashion, rather than summon aggressive energy in order to try to uproot or flatten them.

And yet, as any competent Zen ink painter will be aware, such paintings need not, and will often not, be viewed with the above deeper symbolism in mind.

Thus, a well-rendered Zen ink landscape painting can always be enjoyed simply at face value – as a momentary retreat from the intensity of one's dusty, busy, metropolitan life.

As Qīngyuán's saying goes, then, 'mountains are mountains, waters are waters,' and from their life-affirming aspects – their wholesome natural tendencies, we can receive some inner peace – some noble empowerment and energy, as we hike through our lives and climb our own personal spiritual mountains.

For there are many paths to the top of the proverbial spiritual mountain – famously so, but the view is always the same – namely, that of a naturally asymmetrical physical universe within which we must find a practical, functional internal balance.

Therefore, when there is a wholesome, lively depiction of precarious mountains interspersed with flowing waters hanging on our wall, this profound truth can be remembered all the more often – and especially so if there is also a physical, three-dimensional 'living' Zen landscape of some sort within or nearby our home.

II

THE WAY OF TEA: HYGIENE

Chinese tea has its very own saint – a man called LùYǔ, who wrote the *Classic of Tea* (*ChájĪng* – 茶经) more than one thousand years ago.

In his book, LùYǔ explains that water sourced from wells, large rivers, or turbulent streams is never the best for making tea. Instead, it is better to collect water from the middle of a small mountain river – where it is rippling gently among the rocks.

In this regard, Zen tea drinking, as an act of self-compassion, is as much about the quality of the water as it is about the medicinal tea leaf itself.

For water, in being essential to both the internal and external cleanliness of the body, is a medicine of sorts – with a certain level of hydration being necessary for our kidneys to excrete toxins efficiently.

Thus, Zen tea may be primarily viewed as a hygiene-driven ritual that is guided by our natural intention to remain healthy – partly by helping us to consume sufficient amounts of water throughout the day.

At the very beginning of a Zen tea-drinking session, therefore, the tea set is most often washed clean with a liberal deluge of freshly boiled water – in joyful celebration of the water's presence in our lives.

And even though this splashing, sloshing, and apparent mindless pouring away of good water could look wasteful to an onlooker who is unfamiliar with traditional Chinese tea's Zen background, this aspect of the ritual serves as a way of paying one's respects to the water – of remembering that water is not just something for us to put into or onto our bodies.

For from a broader perspective, water is a deeply profound element that is essential to our ecosystems as a whole. Thus, it can be awarded an appropriate level of recognition via a sacrifice (when it is not scarce of course).

And after this heartfelt appreciation of water has been kindled – with the teaware now clean and pre-warmed, then the tea leaves also tend to be given a quick wash before the brewing ensues – again, with a lively, generous drenching that washes away any dust or germs.

As a result, a tea 'ceremony' has the potential to become quite chaotic, and therefore demands that fine control – a grounded, mindful approach is exercised during the procedure. And yet, if the water use does get a little too lively, then tea cloths are on hand for the mopping-up of spillages – due to an intention on the part of the brewer to keep the tea preparation surface as clean and as empty of clutter as possible.

This emphasis on cleanliness and de-cluttering during Zen tea drinking is not only a physical concern, though, *it is also a mental observance*, which harks back to the ultimate origin of Zen tea – all the way to the Buddhist monasteries of ancient China, where tea was used by monks in particular to refresh their minds as they went about their prescribed tasks.

In fact, it was one such Buddhist task – namely, the requirement for monks to help those who were in need, that led to the introduction of a certain Chinese boy to the path of tea drinking – a boy who was abandoned by his family when very young, and was to become the 'tea saint' known as Lù Yǔ.

For after having been taken into a Zen monastery by the monks, the boy gained a keen interest in the preparation of fresh high quality tea leaves plucked from bushes on the monastery grounds.

Thus, he would offer temple visitors special tea brews – so that they could clear their minds and have a taste of daily monastic practice.

However, this service was not particularly special in and of itself, since such hospitality was standard at Chinese monasteries. And so, it is within this broader cultural context that another famous tea-related Zen story takes place, in fact – involving a Tang Dynasty Chinese Zen master, called Zhàozhōu Cóngshěn (趙州從諗), who was often happy to interact with various

The Way of Tea

visitors and disciples at his monastery – but not in the way that people expected.

Instead, Zhàozhōu would confound his guests and students alike by replying to every enquiry that he received with the following phrase, "Chī Chá Qù"; literally "swallow tea go."

This would become quite a famous Zen koan, even, and is often translated into English as "go have some tea," since the master was apparently encouraging his students to avoid frivolous chatter and instead engage as directly and simply as possible in formal monastic discipline – in their daily routine, which involved drinking tea between scheduled activities.

For although the timetabled tasks at the monastery changed as the day progressed, the most common activity was drinking tea after completing each task, which naturally caused a certain tea-infused ambience to permeate the monks' daily flow.

Thus, even though, as a stimulant, tea serves the purpose of helping the body to metabolise and clean itself out, in formal Zen contexts, tea drinking supports the main goal of cleaning out the mind – of maintaining mental hygiene, which is ultimately accomplished through meditation.

And yet, since any kind of activity can be attended to mindfully, preparing and drinking tea can itself become a meditation – which the fine art of brewing high quality green tea in particular lends itself to.

LùYǔ therefore found *his* particular Way or Dao – a meditative path to Zen enlightenment, that lay in tea preparation and drinking.

For if, when brewing green tea, one is not paying

fine attention to the temperature of the water and the length of each steeping, one can very easily create a bitter infusion, and even waste some high quality leaves – disappointing oneself, as well as any other person who is taking part in the ritual.

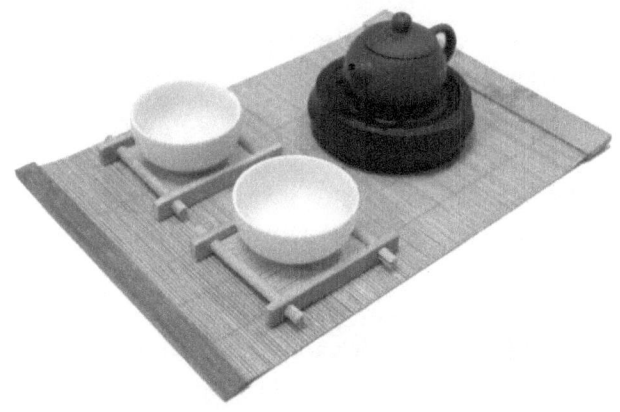

A mindful, meditative mindset is perfect, therefore, for brewing and thoroughly enjoying a cup of medicinal green tea – an act which in turn further invigorates that meditative mindset, creating a positive feedback loop in the process.

In this respect, Chinese Zen tea could be said to be an internal hygiene routine for the mind as well as the body – a holistic detox, which is achieved by honouring the naturally arising intention to irrigate all of one's cells – as an act of heartfelt compassion.

What is more, from this epicentre of fine, noble, self-compassionate intent – from the honoring of one's reflexive wish to clean out both body and mind of toxic content (which includes our ego, of course), it can be found that all of the similar requirements particular to formal mindfulness or Zen meditation practice arise – a sense of moral duty, for example, and the upright seated posture.

For such a dignified posture, in being the most expanded whilst simultaneously relaxed upright stance possible, is the most efficient method of irrigating one's cells with tea – as it is for one's blood circulation in general.

Chinese Zen tea preparation and drinking eventually begins, therefore, just like Zen kung fu, Zen calligraphy, and Zen ink painting, to 'do us,' to an extent – it demands that we change ourselves to a more wholesome posture, or mode of being, in order to appreciate the discipline more thoroughly.

Thus, Japanese people who appreciate Zen tea often talk of 'tea life' – how the enjoyment of formal Zen tea hygiene, polite social etiquette, mindfulness meditation, and of course the consumption of fine beverages, as well as many other positive aspects of the practice, filter through into all of the other rituals in their lives.

For example, a disciplined Zen tea practitioner may find that the area around their domestic tea table begins to become cleaner and clearer – as if ripples of hygiene were emanating from their Zen tea practice into the rest of the house, which in turn affects the clarity of their mind. For an unfinished project left lying around – a loose object without a place to call home, is a problem waiting to be solved, which engages the mind on a subconscious level as one shares the object's space.

As a result, traditional Zen teahouses and domestic tea rooms tend to be impeccably clean – with dirt, dust, and clutter kept literally 'out of sight, out of mind.'

When we honour and celebrate our natural reflexive intention to purge our bodies of pollutants through the regular practice of Zen tea, then, a hygienic chain reaction is begun.

It starts with the manipulation of the tea set, then the water, then the tea, and always involves mastering our bodies and attention.

In this way, a tea ritual becomes a positive life-affirming and reinforcing process, which flows through into the rest of our being and the world around us.

This is because *it just feels good to be cleaner* – a fact that can become increasingly prevalent in our lives as our appetites for Zen arts grow. For even though, when we were children, we often saw mundane daily hygiene rituals – tasks such as brushing our teeth or taking a shower, as chores that we would try to avoid, once we had gotten older, we felt that we could not happily go a day without them.

So Zen tea is not so much about knowing how to brew rare kinds of fermented leaves, or pour tea elegantly, as it is about cultivating and maintaining a self-compassionate state of mind. And when that mind is brought to the fore, then enthusiasm for a more elegant existence, as well as well-brewed tea, arrives as a perfectly natural consequence.

In this regard, Zen tea is in fact an innate aspect of

our condition, and we just need to fetch a tea set, sit down, and allow the water to begin flowing. For once that happens, our reflexive intention to maintain our physical hygiene can support and fuel any inspiration to cultivate *better mental hygiene*.

The act of mindfully brewing and drinking fine tea every day may thus become as easy and enjoyable as brushing one's teeth – an effortless detox ritual that takes place in harmony with our kind and caring true nature.

12

THE WAY OF TEA: SELF

In the *Assutavā Sutta*, Gautama Buddha states that if a person is to believe in a permanent idiosyncratic self – an ego, or 'soul,' then it is better for such an identity to be rooted in the physicality of the body, rather than within the slippery abstractions of the mind.

For Buddhists allocate to the mind four different overlapping and thus highly complex 'aggregate selves' – illusory immortal souls of sorts, that people tend to take refuge within when the pain of their perceived mortality becomes too intense.

These mental selves are a person's identified feelings, perceptions, habituated conditioning, and consciousness – the details of which can be very difficult to discern when we are immersed within the complex affairs of everyday life.

The physical body, on the other hand, presents only one relatively simple self that can be attached to, and that is one's cellular community.

And yet, the Buddha did not know about the existence of cells, of course. He instead referred to the more basic natural elements (in the *Satipatthāna Sutta*, or the *Mahā Rāhulovāda Sutta*, for example) that constitute the physical body – such as earth-like solidity, water-like fluidity, and fire-like heat.

Thus, Gautama taught that a handful of natural elemental qualities combine to create a physical self – a dynamic, ever-changing 'physical aggregate,' mound-like 'heap,' or bundle – an entity that we may (however illogically) label as our 'permanent identity,' which breaks down into its constituent elements after death.

In China, meanwhile, there was another elemental system emerging at that time – the five elemental phase changes of nature, that went on to inform traditional Chinese medicine and other practices.

This ancient Chinese five elements system had broad overlaps with the Buddhist elemental stance, however. And so, the scene was set for the two elemental systems of Buddhism and Chinese medicine respectively to come together and figure something out – a product of which was, arguably, traditional Chinese Zen tea.

For the Tang Dynasty 'tea saint,' LùYǔ, wrote in the fourth chapter of his *Classic of Tea*, that his 'wind stove' – a metal brazier that he used to boil water over a charcoal or wood fire, had the following two sentences written on its legs, 'body balance five elements to remove one hundred diseases' (TǐJūnWǔXíngQùBǎiJí – 体均五行去百疾), and, 'water trigram above, wind trigram below, fire trigram at its centre' (KǎnShàngXùnXiàLíYúZhōng – 坎上巽下离于中).

The trigram elements that he refers to, although all found within the Buddhist elemental system rather than the traditional Chinese five elemental phases system, are three of the basic eight 'BāGuà' trigram symbols that were derived from ancient Chinese binary mathematics, and which are often arranged around a 'yin-yang' symbol for use in fengshui or traditional Chinese medicine.

One can still see those trigrams in use today in a modern international context, even – on South Korea's national flag, where four such trigrams are arranged in a circle around a blue and red 'yin-yang' type graphic.

In ancient China, however, these four bagua symbols, plus four other additional trigrams (which all together form the standard eight bagua), were combined with one another to form a permutation of sixty-four hexagrams.

And these hexagrams, representing the binary numbers zero to sixty-three, were then arranged in a mysterious, seemingly illogical numerical sequence in one of China's oldest and most revered books – the *I-Ching* (YìJīng), or *Book of Changes*.

Interestingly, to this day, no matter the efforts of gifted mathematicians all over the world, there has been no adequate theory to explain the apparently random sequence of numbers in the *I-Ching*, with the seventeenth century European philosopher and mathematician Leibniz being confounded by its numerical code, even – *if there is indeed any such code embedded within it.*

No matter Leibniz's ultimate failure, however, his investigations into the *I-Ching* resulted in him inadvertently inventing the modern binary number system that lies at the heart of our computing technology.

And this profound by-product may not have been as random a result as one might assume, in fact. For the *I-Ching* – literally, '*Changes Classic,*' asserts that within its sequential order of sixty-four hexagrams, there is a deeply practical wisdom – an essential pattern or blueprint, and thus the trace of a particular dynamic flow, that governs all of nature – a sophisticated 'system,' that can deliver deep insights regarding the true nature of life, death, the seasons, the heavens, and the human self.

Thus, the 'tea saint' LùYǔ's second wind stove inscription, which states 'water trigram above, wind trigram below, fire trigram at its centre,' with its inclusion of three of the standard eight bagua trigrams' names, was not merely a statement along the lines of 'when brewing tea, put the water above, wind below, and fire in the middle.' Rather, he was harking back to a very specific esoteric cultural heritage.

For his selection of three key dynamic elements needed for brewing tea – water, wind, and fire, were not labelled with the standard Chinese characters used for such objects. Instead, LùYǔ used the traditional labels *for the bagua trigrams that represent those elements* – words which were more process-orientated in their defining of elemental qualities.

And intriguingly, it was the ancient Chinese Daoist mystics, rather than Chinese Buddhists or Confucians, who were the traditional promoters of these bagua concepts – placing them at the heart of their cosmological system, even – as symbolic guides that informed various rituals and practices, including martial-arts-related and yoga-like exercises.

And yet, these bagua-informed exercises, which were utilised in order to bring about better congruence with the Dao, and required practitioners to focus on and refine the subtle energetic properties of their bodies (an approach which gave rise to a formal practice known as Daoist internal alchemy (NèiDānShù – 内丹术)), were not so different from the practice of formal seated Buddhist meditation.

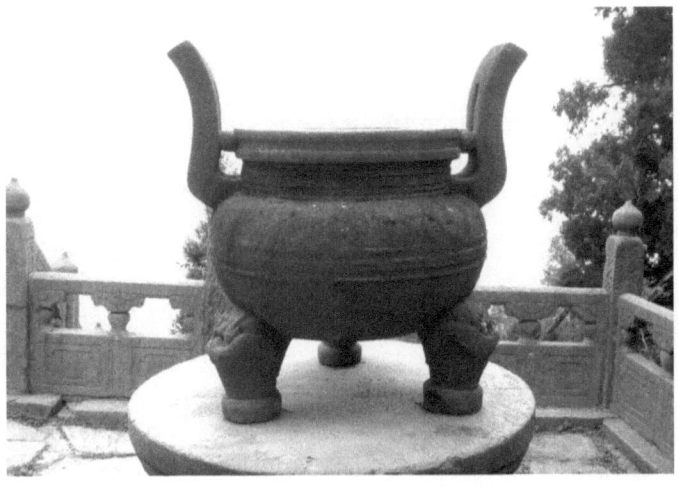

A large stone Dǐng tripod cauldron sculpture located at the legendary home of Daoist martial arts, on Wudang Mountain, China.

Thus, it seems that LùYǔ was explicitly linking the practice of brewing Zen tea to these ancient Daoist alchemical exercises. And this is not so surprising when one considers the fact that the ancient Daoist internal alchemists equated their art with *brewing and refining elixirs* in a tripod cauldron known as a Dǐng (鼎).

For example, in a second century A.D. Daoist inner alchemy text called *Trinity Union Deed* (*CānTóngQì* – 参同契), one finds the following:

> *"The Fire Prescription is not falsely composed.*
>
> *Perform the I-Ching Changes to know them.*
>
> *Supine moon governs the stove and tripod cauldron,*
>
> *White Tiger acts as the brewing centre,*
>
> *Mercurial Sun acts as streaming pearls,*
>
> *Green Dragon with it – all carried together.*
>
> *Hold up East to incorporate West,*
>
> *Dynamic nature and corporeality themselves mutually adhering."*

Self

火	计	不	虚	作
Huǒ	Jì	Bù	Xū	Zuò
(The) Fire	Prescription	is not	falsely	composed

演	易	以	明	之
Yǎn	Yì	Yǐ	Míng	Zhī
perform	*The Changes*	to	know	them

偃	月	法	炉	鼎
Yǎn	Yuè	Fǎ	Lú	Dǐng
supine	moon	governs	stove	(and) tripod cauldron

白	虎	为	熬	枢
Bái	Hǔ	Wéi	Áo	Shū
white	tiger	acting as	brewing	centre

汞	日	为	流	珠
Gǒng	Rì	Wéi	Liú	Zhū
mercurial	sun	acting as	streaming	pearls

青	龙	与	之	俱
Qīng	Lóng	Yǔ	Zhī	Jù
green	dragon	with it	carried	all together

举	东	以	合	西
Jǔ	Dōng	Yǐ	Hé	Xī
hold up	East	to	incorporate	West

魂	魄	自	相	拘
Hún	Pò	Zì	Xiāng	Jū
dynamic nature	(and) corporeality	themselves	mutually	adhering

In fact, in addition to these commonalities that exist between the apparatus and meditative components of ancient Daoist alchemical practices and traditional Chinese Zen tea, there are similarly profound overlaps between such alchemy and formal modern mindfulness and Zen meditation theory.

For example, the Vietnamese Zen master Thich Nhat Hanh likens formal seated Zen meditation to patiently boiling potatoes in a pot, and emphasises the need for active, mindful management in our lives of what he calls 'habit energies' – cyclical biochemically-driven appetites that govern our subconscious 'routines,' or habitual behaviours.

What is more, he admonishes his students to manage these habit energies by befriending and flowing along with them – in order to win their powerful allegiance – mostly by engaging in peaceful belly breathing, whilst smiling warmly – heartfully and compassionately, towards them.

And interestingly, if one takes LùYǔ's sentence, 'water trigram above, wind trigram below, fire trigram at its centre,' as a set of similar instructions for formal mindfulness or Zen meditation, then Nhat Hanh's guidance may be matched quite perfectly.

For the water trigram, 'Kǎn' (坎), refers to a pit or canyon that holds water, and thus overlaps with holding one's awareness empty so that the water-like 'heavenly Way' can be 'channeled.' The wind trigram, Xùn (巽), meanwhile, represents something more like following the fluidity of nature, and therefore overlaps with following the flow of the ancient Chinese qigong breathing all the way down to the belly. And the fire trigram, Lí (离), means to part – like when fire is used to smelt metal and part it from its impurities, which overlaps with prioritising the feeling of one's compassionate 'glowing' Buddhist warm heart over any cold-hearted judgements or unwholesome compulsions that arise.

In this way, we arrive at a basic meditation method that is represented by the three bagua trigrams that LùYǔ emphasised – namely, emptying ones awareness (opening to water above), whilst flowing with abdominal breathing (soothing wind below), and in a thoroughly warm-hearted and therefore compassionate manner (glowing brightly with purifying fire at the centre).

Thus, it seems that LùYǔ, who was alleged to have grown up in a Zen temple and was therefore very familiar with Zen practices and their relatively broad cultural backgrounds, was using the brewing of tea as a metaphor for the essential core of Zen meditation practice and Daoist meditative internal alchemy – all combined into one.

And if this is indeed the case, then one would expect his other inscription, the sentence 'body balance five elements to remove one hundred diseases,' to hold the same profound multi-layered potency – and we are not disappointed.

Because the traditional Chinese five elements (earth, metal, water, wood, and fire) just happen to be tangibly present during a traditional Zen tea session – via the earthenware cups, the metal brazier and kettle, the boiled water, the dried woody tea leaves, and the fire in the stove – all needing to be 'balanced' according to their correct amounts and positions.

However, what is perhaps more profound is that during the brewing process, these elements are coming together harmoniously (via the tea brewer's skill) to create a beverage that, once imbibed, *simultaneously heals and physically becomes our body.*

Therefore, LùYǔ's Zen tea ceremony directly demonstrates traditional Chinese Zen Buddhist theory regarding the physical manifestation of the human form from non-living elements – a process of automatic biological, physical arising, which in turn creates our sentience, and thus our human self-view.

And LùYǔ would not have necessarily been alone in illustrating this profound phenomenon. For other similarly vivid yet less immediate representations of the arising of an impersonal self (what the Japanese Sōtō Zen master Shunryu Suzuki called 'Big Self') are used by Zen teachers to put across the same idea as this dynamic 'elemental bundle' theory.

Thich Nhat Hanh, for example, describes a flower being fed by sunshine, rain clouds, fertile soil, and so on – to the point that it is empty of any flower at all.

It is not completely empty, however – far from it. Rather, it is full of the elements that are interacting to create it, which were ultimately manifested when the stars of our universe exploded. And going back further, those elements were formed when the big bang occurred – and were perhaps present, even, during previous big bangs that are infinite in number.

In any case, Nhat Hanh's above description is simply an expansion of the famous ancient Buddhist *Heart Sutra* statement, 'form is emptiness, and emptiness is form,' which indicates that our form is empty of any inherent self, whilst at the same time that emptiness is itself a potent form, since it is *full of every potential 'self' – full of infinitely interacting infinite forms.*

Such a concept-driven realisation as this is merely a mental gymnastics exercise, though – it can easily be negated as a trivial mind game.

However, if one were to *directly witness* this true nature within and around one during a Zen tea ceremony – *feeling it* as a seamless flow of consumption and consummation, and thus existential arising, then that would be a much more powerful insight.

And so this is where LùYǔ's genius apparently lay. For the ultimate conclusion of such a tea-based practice – especially now that we know our minds arise from the cells that constitute our nervous systems, is that we are indeed truly empty of any inherently permanent or discrete self.

Instead, just like a bright flame miraculously appearing due to a match being struck on the side of a matchbox, this awareness that we identify with personally is merely a meeting of a multitude of *dead yet simultaneously immortal* physiochemical conditions.

For there is in fact no absolute 'struck flame' independent of match, matchbox, and the air around it. Rather, there is just a *cooperative arising of forms* that we like to draw lines between and then label with the words 'match,' 'matchbox,' 'oxygen,' and 'flame.'

In the context of a Zen tea ceremony, however, the labelled forms become 'water,' 'tea,' 'cup,' 'my hand,' 'my mouth,' and so on – all originating from one infinitely spacious, seamless nature.

And this natural, impersonal flow is not so difficult to meet with directly, in fact. For we can literally feel such truth as we follow the tea down our throats – into and through our cells, our nervous system, our skin, kidneys, and so forth.

What is more, when the tea brewing is of high quality, this truth is made much easier to swallow, since the 'heavenly elixir' roots us deeply in the present moment via its potent, delicious 'nectar' – meaning that the more skillful the tea master that brews the tea, the deeper, more pleasant, and thus acceptable the taste of existential truth becomes.

For similarly to mindfulness or Zen meditation, it is all just a matter of how thoroughly – mindfully and 'choicelessly,' we immerse ourselves in and flow along with the whole process – how much we appreciate and literally lose ourselves within 'what is' – within all the harmonious elemental interactions, whilst intending to go beyond the mere ideas of 'elements' and 'interactions' – just engaging as directly (and light-heartedly) as possible with the physical dynamics – the wholesome true nature, that unites all the objects around and within us.

In fact, Buddhists give this simultaneous inter-dependent existence of all objects the term 'co-dependent arising,' which infers that there is a lack of any absolute personal individuality – any essential agency, behind our dynamic automatically manifesting being – something that in turn implies we can just relax, 'let go,' and trust the natural universe to do most of the work of being alive for us.

This truth is even alluded to in formal secular mindfulness instruction at times – when, for example, instructors encourage beginners to actively let go of their breath and trust their biological reflexes – their genetic programming, to take care of their breathing, or to let go into abstract spacious awareness – in the same way that we somehow 'let go' of consciously controlling our lives in order to fall asleep every night.

Thus, the condition – the balance, of our body can be recognised to depend heavily on our mental condition – no matter whether we have drunk any tea or not, and in turn, our mental condition can be recognised to depend heavily on our body. And yet, at the same time, the mind's substrate *is* the body (our neuronal networks), and the body is reflexively influenced by what is perceived by the mind as if it is the truth (our mouth waters, for example, when we imagine chewing on a piece of raw lemon).

So the division between our mind and body is only a pragmatic assertion when discussing these matters – a temporary reference point, in order that one can regain one's bearings – 'get back in the groove', so to speak, of transcending self-ish, divisive concerns.

LùYǔ's first wind stove inscription, then – 'body balance five elements to remove one hundred diseases,' is only a re-minder, a re-setting of a direction – an aiming for a transcendence of a divided and divisive self – towards the domain of a purely elemental balancing act that is operating beyond such words.

Therefore, his reference to the five elements in the first inscription does indeed appear to speak to many different levels of Zen theory and discipline – akin to the second inscription involving the three trigrams, that can seemingly refer to key aspects of brewing Zen tea as well as Daoist internal alchemy practice.

And so, no matter the traditional Chinese five elements and bagua being more Daoist than Buddhist in origin, LùYǔ's inclusion of these profound 'systems' in his book may indeed be useful for fans of Zen tea, or even fans of Zen or mindfulness meditation in general.

In fact, such a blending of Buddhist and Daoist spiritual doctrines involving these elemental forces and the true nature of the mind and body would also occur several hundred years later – during the creation of the famous Chinese classic novel *Journey to the West*, which is an allegory for a spiritual practitioner's journey along the Chinese Zen Buddhist path.

In its beginning chapters, for example, the story outlines the chaotic antics of an impudent monkey king – a metaphor for what Buddhists famously refer to as a person's 'monkey mind,' which is the wilder dimension of the human condition – the part that jumps around anxiously when it predicts a loss of self, and thus a personal death of sorts.

And in *Journey to the West*, in order for this monkey-like spirit to be subjugated – for 'peace to be restored to the heavens,' the Buddha arrives to divest the naughty monkey of his undeserved powers – by imprisoning him beneath a mountain composed of the individual non-living fundamental components, or 'energies' – the traditional Chinese five elements, that combine to create a person's physical form.

These phasic energies, which are non-Buddhist in origin, are nevertheless utilised by the Buddha in order to serve as proof that the monkey's fear of his perceived death – of his physical living form disappearing, is not founded in the observation of any true natural law.

Rather, the Buddha 'evidences' to the monkey that

since the fundamental elements that create monkeys or humans can never disappear from existence (they merely transform and interact indefinitely), then birth and death must be illusory events.

The monkey, trapped under this profound 'mountain' of empirical insight, thus finds himself unable to move onwards in his anxiety-driven mischief – he is literally stopped in his tracks by the Buddha's enlightened logic.

And so, this colourfully depicted event clearly, or perhaps entertainingly, represents the Buddhist reasoning (as has already been thoroughly explored in this chapter) that our body, and thus our physical self, is merely a dynamic, ever-changing aggregate of various non-living phasic elemental conditions originating in nature, and is therefore ultimately immortal.

Thus, at the end of the story, the monkey king, along with the Buddhist monk that he is accompanying and protecting, achieves buddhahood – only after accepting with his whole being, however, that there is no true permanent self or ego, and therefore no true death – *because there is no 'one' to die*.

There is, instead, just a constant ongoing combining and separating of 'already dead' co-interacting elements – what we today know to be carbon, hydrogen, iron, calcium, oxygen, and so on, that aggregate to form our bodies and minds.

And it seems that it was an experience of precisely this kind of truth that LùYǔ intended to facilitate for the tea-drinker – namely, *a direct experience of their own elementally-dependent arising, and thus direct evidence of an absolute impersonality to their being* – by way of a peaceful, meditative appreciation of Zen tea 'alchemy.'

For such insight would arrive from beyond words – visually, as well as *metabolically* – within the more 'true' spacious domain of buddha, 'the land of satori,' where the five elements work their 'magic,' and the tea master, or master-in-the-making, skillfully – mindfully, balances external elements in order to balance his or her body's internal elements, and vice versa.

Thus, traditional Chinese Zen tea practice is so steeped in the wisdom of Zen teachings that after it appeared in China it was difficult for a person not to be profoundly changed after attending even one session with a good tea master.

LùYǔ's book therefore became an officially recognised classic text – branded as a *Jīng*, to be placed alongside the teachings of LaoTzu, Confucius, and the Buddha.

And it was even carried over to Japan, as well as many other East Asian countries, where new Zen tea fans indulged in the wholesome enjoyment of flowing along with their compassionate nature – selflessly experiencing the various naturally arising elements combining harmoniously to create a pure, seamlessly positive sense of cosmic being.

A famous Chinese saying goes, therefore, 'Chá Chán Yī Wèi' (茶禅一味) – literally 'tea and Zen one flavour.' For an emptied teacup, just like a mind emptied of self, is, during an authentic Zen tea session, tangibly full of the potency of the whole universe – and that is a wonderful thing to partake in.

13

THE WAY OF TEA: FLOW

From a traditional Chinese medicine perspective, drinking hot water is an indispensable practice for maintaining good health, since it promotes the circulation of 'Qì' (气) and blood, and thus flushes out stagnation.

In fact, the concept of qi pervades all traditional Chinese health systems, but it is most often encountered in western contexts as a result of qìgōng (or kigong/chikung) practitioners promoting their art.

Still, the subtleties of universal qi dynamics are not necessarily agreed upon by every Chinese person.

In its simplest conception, however, qi is merely organic energy or momentum flowing within the body, which can be influenced by the activity of one's conscious mind.

For example, if you scan through your body with your attention, you may notice that your leg has gone dead, or your shoulders are raised up uncomfortably. And in order to relieve those symptoms, you will tend to *make the conscious decision to relax and open* those stagnant areas, thus allowing energy to once again move throughout your physical system more efficiently.

And this can happen on increasingly finer levels of muscular activity – within the stomach and the face, for example, and deep within the hips, to the point that wherever one's attention goes, that area relaxes and opens up more, and fresher energy arrives.

This mechanism can be further enhanced, even – by allowing the breathing process to massage one's abdomen from above, after which one may consciously encourage the soothing waves created by that modulation to constantly travel through the body as far as possible.

As a formal health maintenance practice, this approach seems to have been a very widespread one, in fact – known to a variety of cultures all over the world. For example, it apparently gave rise to some of the 'breath work' components found within traditional Indian yoga, as well as Chinese qigong – where one practices 'breathing into one's limbs,' and so on.

Thus, the word 'Qì,' when used by Chinese people, tends to refer to phenomena related to the air or breath, but it can also mean vital energy, spirit, or even the weather. For dreary weather tends to dampen our spirits, and as nearly every British person can testify, there's nothing like a cup of hot tea to blast away the grey clouds hovering over one's head!

And yet, when drinking tea is not possible or appropriate, then mindful body scan exercises can serve a similar purpose, since they can encourage one's whole system to open up more – as one scans through one's body warm-heartedly, and 'breathes into' any discomfort that is detected.

In this regard, a secular mindfulness body scan meditation is in fact a very simple qigong practice, no matter one's stance on all this mysterious qi business.

For the most practical benefit that arises from exploring 'qi dynamics' is the emphasis on maintaining fluid, unimpeded energy flow – to literally go with the flow of the body's natural chemical disposition, which can include a person's outward physical behavior, of course – as we see in arts such as tai chi.

Unfortunately, for us post-natal highly socialised humans, this ideal harmony between our 'qi system' and lifestyle is not something that tends to occur naturally, however. Because after birth, the wholesome biological processes that existed within our bodies before we were born were covered up as we began to mature – as we became self-aware, and thus conditioned by self-ishness.

The stubborn ego that we must develop as part of our sophisticated social 'programming' becomes our curse, therefore – it causes our muscles to remain contracted for longer than necessary, for example, which leads to excessive triggering of our sympathetic nervous systems – something that in turn can create various imbalances, and thus stagnations and obstructions, within our circulatory systems.

Drinking hot water, then – with or without tea leaf components in it, is part of a traditional Chinese health practice that aims to loosen up toxic internal tension – by melting away energy blockages, and therefore bringing our whole being into better harmony with our true nature.

For once this more wholesome condition begins to arrive, we may more easily overcome the restrictive aspects of our egos, and thus better maintain a more warm-hearted perspective – rather than grow frosty and bitter about our situation.

In fact, all Zen arts aim for this socially-congruent ideal, regardless of whether the practitioner is alone or in company. And so, when brewing a hot beverage of the Zen variety by oneself, it is always prepared mindfully – warm-heartedly, as if good friends were present.

Because no matter how far up and across any cloud-obscured mountain you may have climbed in order to be free from the dusty, busy world, it seems that you can never be *truly* alone – since your mind itself is composed of a network of highly socialised communicating neurons (and thus a community) – before we even start to consider all of the other kinds of cells that contribute cooperatively to your ongoing being in this universe.

When no other human is present, then, our bodily cells become our honoured guests – the recipients of our humble service. And when we are in more traditional company, well, there are just more cells present to cater for.

That being so, there are certain outward gestures and movements of the body, of course, that communicate whether our condition of mind – our stream of consciousness, is flowing in congruence or conflict with other minds. Thus, when we are in the company of other people, there tends to be more inspiration to be mindful of one's social etiquette – what Confucius referred to as respectful politeness.

As has already been inferred in a previous chapter, however, polite etiquette need not be induced via a set of imposed, rigid formal rules. Rather, if one is recognising the truth regarding the considerable economic benefit of genuine prosocial intent – of expressed 'innate virtue' and compassion, then polite respect and the outward behaviours that communicate such a civil stance will manifest spontaneously as one flows along with the tea brewing and serving process – as they do, for example, upon a person assuming a seated meditation posture that embodies dignity.

And perhaps unsurprisingly, therefore, a Zen tea ceremony unfolds in harmony with the Chinese Buddhist bodhisattva ideal – namely, to kindle a deeply heartfelt prosocial intent to help all sentient beings – by a practitioner vowing not to enter Nirvana without all those beings coming along for the ride.

This aim is never to be achieved through proselytising or through covert manipulation tactics, however. Instead, it is to be satisfied by merely *being of service* – being politely supportive of 'what is,' and thus supportive of the human prosocial predisposition and the economic potency of that stance.

Embedded within our broader civil existence, then, there is a tangible social contract – an inescapable social responsibility, that we must honour if we wish to feel comfortable and flow along harmoniously within our societies.

And this phenomenon can be witnessed very clearly in any secular society when, for example, children enjoy hosting tea parties of sorts on behalf of their toys or friends.

Thus, there is nothing special or supra-mundane about Zen tea, for it is just an expression of what Zen teachers call 'everyday mind,' or 'universal mind' – the mind or heart that is common to all humans, which instinctively seeks to satisfy its basic daily needs.

For the act of drinking water is simply an essential daily ritual, and hot water can boost our spirits – especially so when tea leaf components are mixed into it.

In this respect, Zen tea can therefore become a powerful part of one's daily flow – effortlessly so. Because as one follows along with one's wholesome intentions and the path of the water, and thus finds more harmony with the ever-changing fluid universe, one's own true nature can be more deeply appreciated – along with other peoples' natures also, allowing one to more effortlessly enjoy hosting or taking part in a fine tea ritual in the spirit of mutual service.

And this is the key, in fact, to accessing what psychologists refer to as 'the flow state' – an impersonal process-oriented enjoyment of the present moment that manifests beyond time, boredom, and anxiety.

For it involves just mindfully *being*, and appreciating that 'ride' – as skills competently meet challenges, thus giving rise to a finely tuned attention-dependent balancing act that generates significant existential nourishment.

In the case of Zen tea, this fine balancing act manifests as a maintaining of hygiene in body and mind, which in turn allows one to more competently prepare and drink good quality tea – without over- or under-steeping, or scalding the tea leaves.

And with some dedicated practice, a Zen tea host can eventually become so engaged with the flow of the water, the heating, the leaves, the teacups, and the wholesome peaceful celebration of being and becoming – inter-mingling with and manipulating the fundamental elements of nature, as well as being of service to others, that he or she is no longer consciously self-oriented or time-aware.

Instead, one is just being One – bigger, broader, expanded, infinitely co-mingled with the tea, the tea set, and every unique moment that arises, from one cup being filled and emptied to the next – just flowing in harmony with the magnificence and the mystery of this relentlessly fluid universe.

EPILOGUE:

ZEN ARTS AS A PATH

The Sōtō Zen master Shunryu Suzuki taught that Zen should not cause excitement. In fact, as a practice, it requires just the opposite response – to cool down and calm down, so that one can enjoy the more subtle, and thus finer aspects of one's existence.

In this respect, a Zen lifestyle aims towards an easy appreciation of being, rather than any kind of ecstatic mania.

It seems, however, that such a wholesome aspiration tends to be counter to the kind of ideal life that most people envision. For the majority of men and women on our planet would perhaps prefer to endure a life full of ups and downs – an exciting white-knuckle rollercoaster ride, that makes their heart beat with passion and drama.

And yet, such an existence surely requires constant intense stimulation, even if that means creating drama where there is none to begin with – a lifestyle allegedly described by the first patriarch of Zen, Bodhidharma, as 'painting tigers and dragons for entertainment, and then jumping back in fear of them.'

For even though real tigers and reptiles once posed a considerable threat to our existence, now our potential dangers are much fewer, meaning that most of our perceived threats tend to be self-created – as a result of the way we habitually engage with the world.

In this light, then, if we do indeed wish to pursue a more peaceful existence by using mindfulness or Zen arts, these practices need to be installed in our lives in a way that replaces habitual indulgences in drama and other toxic vices – any revelling in 'cheap thrills.'

Traditionally, such a goal is achieved by embedding daily mind and body unification rituals within some form of spiritual path – a *Way*, or Dao, that is walked, ideally, during every minute of every day.

For the dedicated mindfulness or Zen practitioner seeks to obtain his or her daily happiness not from indulging desires, competitive tendencies, or the temporary blisses of ignorance, but rather from more wholesome sources – such as *the mutual sharing with, and supporting of, one another, and therefore appreciating distributing and receiving loving kindness.*

Thus, a more mindful life begins with the disciplined cultivation of compassion – most often by kindling kindness towards our innermost selves. And this may be achieved through practicing formal self-compassion mindfulness meditation, for example – so that our tangible warm-heartedness may then be able to more effectively and consistently overflow into the world around us – to our families, friends, colleagues, and beyond.

But we cannot just sit at home all day immersed in the self-soothing waves of our breathing – in the womb-like 'void' of inner peace, even if we want that condition to be our standard experience for the rest of our lives.

For our primary focus must be placed elsewhere at times – as we exercise, for example, or communicate, visit a variety of natural surroundings, hydrate and refresh ourselves, socialise, and so on.

And so this is where the Zen arts described in this book can be of great value, since they can help us to meet the above necessary conditions in a way that deeply satisfies our natural intention to sustain our dignity, our health, and to use our energies in the most efficient manner as we go about our daily routines .

Thus, the traditional Zen arts of medieval China were not mere hobbies, and nor were they eccentricities only appreciated by a few elitist individuals. They were, instead, recognised as being necessary for the sustenance of civilised society in general.

For example, Confucius emphasised the practice of the 'six arts of the perfect gentleman' (LiùYì – 六艺), which comprised the performance of rites, music, archery, charioteering, calligraphy, and mathematics.

And after the deeper establishment of Chinese Zen

Buddhist culture during the Tang Dynasty, the more militaristic aspects of the six gentlemanly arts were dropped in favour of honing painting skills, as well as mastering the strategic yet highly complex board game called 'go.'

As a result, a new combination of civil disciplines replaced the six arts of the perfect gentleman – namely, the 'four arts of the scholarly gentleman' (SìYì – 四艺).

And yet, no matter these changes, what ultimately united, and continues to unite, all of these arts into something more than a handful of pastimes, was the body of classical Chinese literature – the ancient philosophical texts, which guided these scholars in the *Way* that the arts were to be practiced for optimal achievement and appreciation.

In fact, this Way, when localised to the human domain, was originally defined by Confucius as 'The Way of the First Kings' (XiānWǎngZhīDào – 先王之道).

For those first rulers of ancient China – the legendary founders of its civilised long-term survival strategy, were described as deeply virtuous individuals. This was on account of their recognition of the significant economic benefits of *benevolence*, which is Rén (仁), in Chinese – its written character being a combination of a human, or person (人), and the number two (二). In other words, it is a visual representation of two people engaging in win-win cooperative strategies.

For example, an ancient Chinese farmer could obtain a fuller belly for himself and his dependents, as well as enjoy a more robust territorial defense strategy, all as a result of joining efforts with another farmer – by benevolently taking part in agricultural teamwork outside of his family group.

And the more heads and hands (not to mention paws, claws, and hooves) that became involved in such win-win interactions, the greater the collective benefits were, of course.

What is more, the larger the food surpluses generated by such cooperatives, the larger the number of specialist jobs – restaurateurs, bakers, and royal chefs, for example, that could be supported, which in turn led to a variety of sophisticated and delicious cuisines being developed and appreciated.

It was just basic economic activity taking place according to the directly observable laws of nature – where many hands worked together in order to make the task of staying alive a lighter job for all.

Whilst in the pursuit of this noble, ancient Way, however, Confucius pointed out that his aspirations towards 'kingly virtue,' and thus his practice of cultivating that prosocial condition, arose primarily from his surrendering to the socioeconomic laws as they existed in nature – *in the heavens*, and therefore beyond the human realm of limited spoken words.

The *ultimate* Way of persisting, then, for Confucius, was the Way prescribed to us by the heavens – by the laws of physics, which was a perspective that LaoTzu also agreed with, it seems.

These sages' main focus, therefore, was not to merely emulate the outward form of previous kings, but rather to discern the subtle, 'devilish' details of

Epilogue

physical nature that those kings were concerned with – the details that governed potentially deadly catastrophes, for example, as well as how to avoid suffering such misfortunes unnecessarily.

As a result, LaoTzu tended to advocate for smaller, more peaceful states than Confucius – where there was more space, and thus more direct contact with the subtleties of nourishing and wise 'mother nature.'

The Confucians, on the other hand, seemed to be more concerned with the administration of much larger and growing states – where direct contact with mother nature was intermingled with complex social affairs directed by state officials. For it seems inevitable that wealthy states will, and can, naturally develop in these more sophisticated and sprawling directions.

In order to better manage such states, then, Confucius sought to emphasise a primarily ethics-driven lifestyle that operated within a domain of being where the tangible truth of our cosmic laws was the main focus, and especially so for those who possessed the greatest power, and thus greatest responsibility.

He would therefore cultivate a sincere commitment to the natural economic truth of 'what is' – through a practice of what he called 'no self-deception' (WúZìQī – 毋自欺), which was itself maintained via an unquenchable appetite for the study of nature's patterns.

We know this, because, in a famous Confucian text called '*Dàxué*' (大学) – '*Great Learning*' (which is the term used for a Chinese university today), the details of the process that allegedly led the first Chinese kings

Zen Arts as a Path

to a more virtuous condition were described as follows (in *The Confucian Book of Rites* (*Lǐjì* – 禮記), Chapter 42, Verse 2):

> "...they first cultivated their moral lives, and upon desiring to cultivate their moral lives, first they corrected their hearts, and upon desiring to correct their hearts, first they made their intentions sincere, and upon desiring to make their intentions sincere, first they broadened their knowledge – broadened it by investigating nature's objects."

先	修	其	身	
Xiān	Xiū	Qí	Shēn	
first	cultivated	their	moral lives	

欲	修	其	身	者
Yù	Xiū	Qí	Shēn	Zhě
and desiring	to cultivate	their	moral lives	;

先	正	其	心	
Xiān	Zhèng	Qí	Xīn –	
first	corrected	their	hearts/minds	

欲	正	其	心	者
Yù	Zhèng	Qí	Xīn	Zhě
and desiring	to correct	their	hearts/minds	;

Epilogue

先	诚	其	意	
Xiān	Chéng	Qí	Yì –	
first	made sincere	their	intentions	

欲	诚	其	意	者,
Yù	Chéng	Qí	Yì	Zhě,
and desiring	to make sincere	their	intentions	;

先	致	其	知
Xiān	Zhì	Qí	Zhī
first	extended	their	knowledge

致	知	在	格	物.
Zhì	Zhī	Zài	Gé	Wù.
extended	knowledge	in	investigating	natural objects

Thus, we find within Confucius' words an apparent admonishment to investigate the laws of nature, with the aim of causing the sincere truth to come to light – in particular the truth that all socialised human beings possess an inherent intention to 'correct their hearts,' and therefore their lives in general.

And as it happens, this is the exact intention of secular mindfulness in our modern times.

So it is perhaps of no surprise, therefore, that right at this very moment, 2500 years after the great sage was alive, westerners who are taking a very similar approach to Confucius (or the ancient 'good kings' that he sought to emulate) are producing the kinds of results that dazzled Confucius' peers.

For in our modern societies, depressive relapses are being halved, and thus peoples' hearts/minds are being 'corrected,' all simply due to the scientific practice of 'extending one's knowledge in investigating nature' –

through the exercising of *mindful curiosity*.

And this 'correction' arrives, because, as is already inferred above, being an 'eternal scholar' of sorts leads to one eventually identifying one's inherent intent to survive efficiently and flexibly as being present within every living organism's makeup – an intent, which, in the case of humans, can then be confidently 'made sincere' – into an *actualised* reflexively prosocial intent, a tangibly manifested human 'Yì' (the very same yi of *yi*quan Zen kung fu and xie*yi* Zen ink painting).

For no matter such prosocial intent arriving from beyond thoughts or words, it can be detected easily enough within our hearts *as a conscience*, and thus a foundation for the cultivation of greater human virtue.

What is more, when Confucius later describes in more detail how to be sincere in one's intentions as a civil human being, he concludes with an explanation of what the economic and psychic rewards of such an investment in sincerity tend to be (Verse 3):

"Wealth decorates a house,

and virtue decorates a person –

with mind broad and body full,

therefore gentlemen must make their intentions sincere."

富	润	屋
Fù	Rùn	Wū
wealth	decorates	a house

Epilogue

德	润	身
Dé	Rùn	Shēn
virtue	decorates	personhood

心	广	体	胖
Xīn	Guǎng	Tǐ	Pán
heart/mind	broad	(and) body	full

故	君	子
Gù	Jūn	Zǐ
therefore	gentleman	persons

必	诚	其	意
Bì	Chéng	Qí	Yì
must	make sincere	their	intentions

Here, it seems that Confucius is dangling the win-win economic carrot – a prize harvest grown from the soil of virtue, and thus intends to attract his audience to the idea of being sincere in their innate civil intentions. For he is promising a more efficient route to material abundance, social respect, a resilient heart, and a nourished, satisfied belly. And what more could a person hope for in life?

Thus, the Confucian six gentlemanly arts, as well as the later four scholarly gentleman's arts, in being guided on the Way by virtue-driven Confucian ethical standards, were all intimately fused with the process of realising the above ideal.

As a result, the Confucian arts lent one another insights and skills that became like four legs of a chair – a practically-rooted spiritual seat upon which a scholar could enjoy a more efficient and wholesome life.

And for those scholars who had more Buddhist or Daoist inclinations, Zen tea and kung fu yoga would become similar lifestyle assets, with the physical postures and use of practical metaphors within all of these disciplines eventually blending together to the point that they ended up as one distilled, refined, unified culture called Chinese 'Zen.'

In this light, then, the greater the number of Zen arts that one practices, the clearer the Zen path becomes in general – especially in its most practical traditional motifs, as well as in how it overlaps with Confucianism, Daoism, and Chinese Buddhism.

And of course, such insight can also inform one's understanding of western secular mindfulness. For all of these arts are one prosocial way at their core – a highly simple, tangible, yet clever approach to survival.

At the same time, however, they are a path that is beyond true verbal definition – a relatively sophisticated way of staying alive, that is certainly not the *only* way, even though it tends to be the most efficient, and thus *wise* way for socialised humans.

My traditional Chinese zen calligraphy teacher, Paul Wang, has, during his lifetime, therefore learned and practiced (and continues to teach) a variety of traditional Chinese zen arts in addition to zen calligraphy – disciplines such as tai chi, qigong, seated zen meditation, and zen tea.

And Paul's wife, Jasmine Zhang, who also practices those arts alongside him, as well as traditional Indian yoga, teaches zen ink painting and hosts zen poetry

Epilogue

reading events.

Meanwhile, my yiquan senior teacher, Cuī Ruìbīn, has extensive knowledge of traditional Chinese medicine, classical Chinese philosophy, a variety of traditional Chinese martial arts, and drinks traditionally prepared Chinese teas daily. He also has many yiquan disciples who practice other Zen arts – such as calligraphy and Buddhist meditation.

Thus, at the Yiquan Academy, I was taught by a coach there that the sense of 'air friction' particular to yiquan exercises – a sensation akin to a tree branch flexibly resisting the force of the wind, may be utilised in order to write traditional Chinese calligraphy more competently.

Similarly, Paul Wang teaches that the prosocial 'Yì' – the natural intent of the virtuous human heart that is harnessed by yiquan practitioners, needs to be visible in the organic shapes of zen calligraphy strokes, and that the qi flow of qigong needs to be visible in the traces that a zen calligraphy brush leaves on paper.

Meanwhile, Jasmine Zhang teaches that the calligraphy brush strokes used to render the elements of a zen ink painting need to be lively – to have the springy, wholesome, life-affirming spirit similar to that manifested by Zen kung fu movements – taking inspiration from the lively 'Yì' of animals and plants.

And so, in these ways, all of the traditional Chinese Zen arts cross-pollinate and inform one another – causing them to deliver practitioners to the same place that formal secular mindfulness does – to an immersion in the positive nature of being human, so that we may flow more in harmony with that condition.

And this does not mean that the teachers or the students of these arts are more enlightened in a Zen Buddhist way than any other person. For all that they really gain insight into by becoming familiar with these practices are standard ancient recipes that can be adapted depending on what is available in the refrigerator of their lives, and some refrigerators are stocked more generously than others. That is just the way it is.

In any case, as Shunryu Suzuki mentioned, to practice Zen is not a lofty or competitive intellectual exercise. Rather, it is more akin to baking bread – to following a basic recipe, over and over again – through actively cultivating a spirit of repetition.

Thus, even though during one's lifetime one may never bake the most perfect bread, and the bread that other people bake may taste better, what is more important and perfect is the *persistence* in the practice day after day – *the discipline* of just doing it, no matter how one feels from one session to the next.

Because it is that process itself that generates the deepest insight, and therefore a considerable increase in one's optimism – one's potential to meet future adverse conditions with confidence, as one begins to consider oneself a kind of 'master in the making.'

In fact, any persistence in a practice always depends upon a vision of mastery, as well as the discipline necessary to achieve that vision within one's lifetime – a factor which, in turn, requires a fine understanding of the human heart – all of its obstacles and passions. And the more one understands about one's heart, the more empowered one becomes, because knowledge – experience, is always empowering.

As a result, mindfulness teachers tend to encourage their students to meditate on a daily basis, by saying, "you don't have to like it, you just have to do it." And after several weeks of dedicated discipline, practitioners come to appreciate the increased mental hygiene that such a practice delivers, and they begin to increasingly depend on its wholesome qualities.

Thus, when a formal mindfulness practice of any sort snowballs, and one's days become increasingly happy, any daydreams about Zen enlightenment no longer matter so much. For any idea – *any mere concept*, of enlightenment that a person possesses before it actually occurs, is wrong. So why worry about it when one can peacefully enjoy aspects of nature in the here and now – possibly whilst resting within an enlightened condition, even, just not bothered enough to check if it is real or not?

For in light of the above, all discipline is 'zen practice' in a sense – it ultimately leads, via dogged persistence and the insight that accumulates along that 'infinite Way,' to buddhahood – saintliness, sageliness, or whatever label one wishes to use, because all solid discipline depends upon the mastering of the human condition.

However, traditional Chinese Zen in particular had the additional benefit of inheriting the most refined wisdom from across the globe – as ancient Greek and Persian culture had mixed with Buddhism on the Indian subcontinent, allowing for the resultant synthesis, 'Greco-Buddhism,' to travel smoothly into

China along the Silk Roads.

Thus, the ancient Chinese native practical wisdom traditions profited from combining their own insights with others that originated from beyond their borders – causing China to become awash in a highly rich international wisdom 'soup' that other civilisations either did not have access to, did not have the appetite for, or just could not manage to concoct on their own.

For history can tell us that Chinese Zen emerged *during a flow of trade and pilgrimage that went more East than West* – as Tang Dynasty China was the most developed and powerful global economy at that time.

Therefore, China's relatively advanced cultural 'golden era' was not necessarily about ethnicity or national politics, it was just the direction in which the winds of human fortune were blowing; namely, eastward – something that was destined to change in favour of the West as the centuries rolled on.

In this context, then, traditional Chinese Zen arts, although having a strong 'Chinese' cultural flavour to them, are, just like the 'western sciences,' *ultimately a global inheritance* – owed to, and now available to, every nation on the planet, and especially so when served up as secular mindfulness practices, rather than specifically Buddhist, Daoist, or East Asian culture.

And this perspective endures, it seems, in the spirit of Gautama Buddha's original teachings, even. For he had no apparent interest in discussing any localised metaphysical assumptions, let alone religious or cultural politics.

Rather, Gautama was only concerned with helping individuals find liberation from suffering – via what

Epilogue

came to be known as his 'Four Noble Truths' – the facts that there is suffering involved in being born (having a

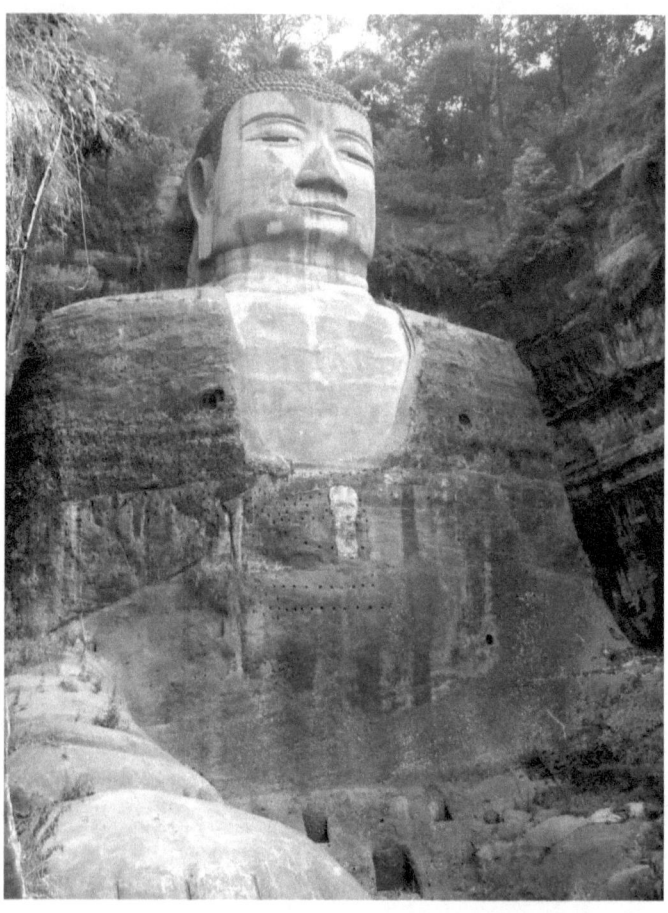

The LeShan Giant Buddha, southwestern China. It is the world's largest present-day stone-cut Buddha. It was built by a Chinese Zen monk during the Tang Dynasty. The tradition of depicting the Buddha in life-like human form, as seen here, was begun by the Greeks who settled in Gandhara – in an area which is now on the border between what we call Afghanistan and Pakistan.

self), there is a specific cause to that suffering (clinging, or attachment), the suffering can end when we flow in harmony with our true nature ('letting go'), and that such a liberation is arrived at if one follows an increasingly wholesome – peaceful and loving, lifestyle.

Thus, religion is, and was, a separate matter to that activity, and is most often not in conflict with secular mindfulness psychology, in any case. For who can disagree, at the end of the day, with the amplification of broad-minded prosociality – with an increase in the presence of warm-heartedness, and therefore love and kindness, in our lives?

And so, traditional Chinese Zen arts, in being steeped in a mixture of Confucianism, Daoism, and Buddhism – not to mention other influences (ancient Greek and Zoroastrian culture, for example), are not covert indoctrinations into any mystical cult or metaphysical belief system. In a sense, they are the complete opposite of that – they are about increasing one's psychological freedoms.

However, at the same time they are most often not in conflict with any such beliefs, in any case. For just like the practice of mindfulness itself, these Zen arts are merely tools that can help us survive more efficiently – more prosocially, in the same way that our brains, limbs, fingers and toes support our civil efforts – the left hand helping the right hand, and vice versa, *in harmony with our universal true nature.*

So no matter our ideas about our existential purpose and origins, our bodies will work in the same

Epilogue

ways – something illustrated by, for example, how the outcomes of mixed martial arts (MMA) bouts speak directly to people via the language of pure physical action, transcending any creed or mysticism in the process, and therefore teaching us that the natural

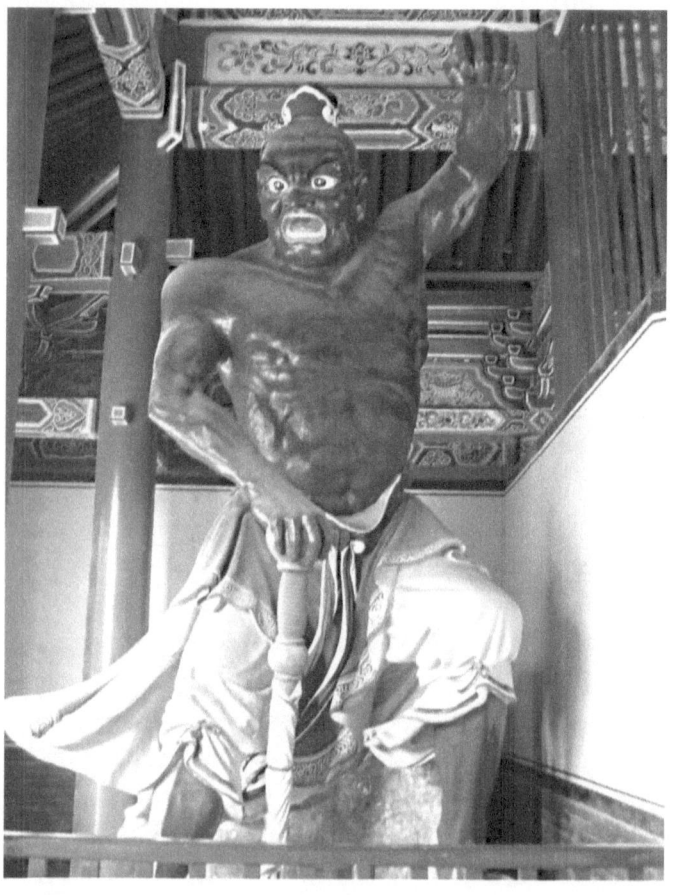

An imposing Vajra protective deity placed at the entrance to Shaolin Temple, China. Similarities between these figures and apparent depictions of the Greek hero Heracles in Gandharan Greco-Buddhist

Zen Arts as a Path

art (presented as being the 'bodyguard' of the Buddha) have been widely noted by scholars.

physical laws of the heavens and the earth are the ultimate deciders of our fates.

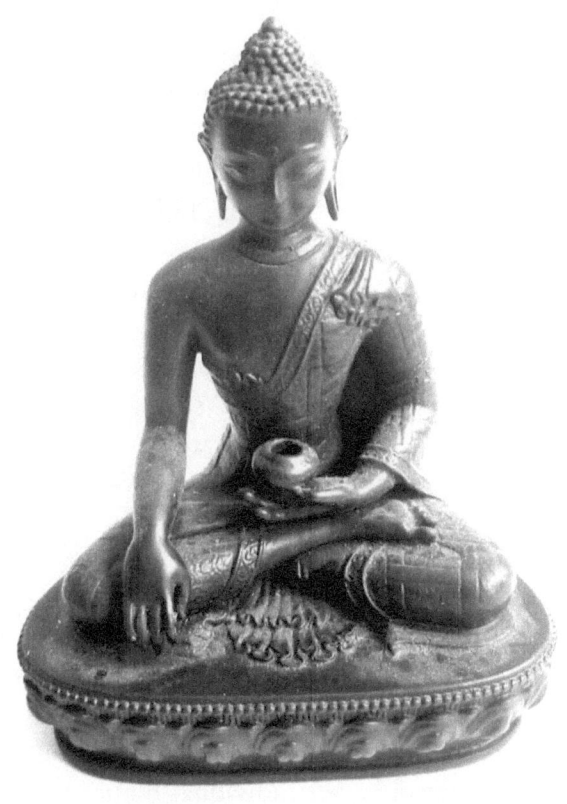

A bronze statue of Gautama Buddha touching the earth – calling it as his witness, in order to ground his insight in the empirical truth of Nature.

Thus, as Gautama Buddha experienced his

enlightenment, he touched the earth below him as his witness – *as proof*, in order to source a practical, tangible, stable, undeniable authority on his experience – *a source originating from beyond slippery words or thoughts* – beyond the mere idea of 'beyond.'

When we feel that we are going to war with the forces of chaos, then, we can 'get wise' to this truth – the laws of the earth and the heavens that decide our fates (and therefore our biophysical situation), and tune into our inherent natural intention to survive fluidly and resiliently – our billions-of-years-old success story that is our autopoiesis.

And this can be done regardless of any questions we may have concerning how or why that process began (if it ever did have a beginning) in order to just borrow its qualities – its expansive, lively springiness and ever-adaptive self-regeneration, so that we may obtain the greatest empowerment available to us – the greatest resilience, when meeting adversity.

For whether we want to frame it so or not, our biological situation *is* a constant battle. But not against other creatures anymore, really. Instead, it is a 'battle' against the tendency that our universe has towards disorder – towards what the German physicist Hermann von Helmholtz called 'a final heat death.'

For it is not only our individual bodies that must eventually die, but also even the current energetic dynamism of this whole universe, it seems – perhaps for a new universe to be born afterwards.

We cannot even hope to live on eternally through our biological descendants, or the 'memes' that we produce, therefore. And so it is imperative for us to relax into what inherent resilience we already possess, and appreciate this life whilst we can – the unique smiles of our family members, for example, as well as those of our friends, and colleagues, and so on – all the people whom we share our civil contract with. Because if we do not, then we risk approaching the ends of our lives – our dissipation into disorder, feeling that we have not yet appreciated this universe enough – our hearts filled with regrets, and thus longing to be able to re-live all of those moments that passed us by.

In this regard, we are not only born into cooperative relationships with other humans, creatures, and plants, we are also born into a 'contract' with the universe – an unspoken agreement to honour 'what is' with our full attention.

For our social laws originate from the same practical cosmos as that of our physical laws – with our physics-driven world needing to be approached in the same way as we do our social world; namely politely and respectfully – mindfully, if we do not want to experience more friction, and thus suffering, than we can manage.

This makes the noble practice of civil virtue relevant, therefore, to our basic existential situation, no matter whether we are a lonesome hermit, or a street vendor in a busy metropolitan city.

And yet, such a polite, socially harmonious condition of being can only truly arise if our human predispositions towards prosocial behaviour are triggered often enough through our enjoyment of the tangible truth of human prosocial economics – through regular first-hand experiences of receiving significant earthly gains as a result of our cooperative efforts.

For in the simpler ancient past, such economic reward pathways were apparently more easily discerned – for example, when we became an extra crop-harvester, an extra pair of eyes, or an extra spear – as part of a broader community, and thus gained very tangible extra potential to defend ourselves and our families from starvation and attack as a result.

In our modern, more technologically advanced societies, however, social media, as well as the increasing automation of basic resource acquisition and production methods, are stripping away our opportunities to *directly witness and feel* the economic benefits of prosociality, which leaves the door open for widespread parasitism to arise in the name of what may seem to be greater efficiency.

And yet, even when we recognise this situation for what it is, attempting to rebalance our communities by merely reading or thinking – *dictating*, ourselves into a more prosocial condition is not enough.

For as the Vietnamese Zen master Thich Nhat Hanh says, one must *engage directly with the world* and make one's recipes for a more virtuous life become an actual pudding – so that the truth, the proof of advantageous prosociality, may be tasted regularly by oneself as well as anyone else who is interested – so that it may be championed as part of an *ongoing socially coherent broadly functional, practical lifestyle*.

For example, one of the most effective fundamental prosocial practices can be to immerse oneself in family duties and enjoy the efficient rewards of cooperation in that context – such as when helping one's parents to clean and cook. And this was exactly the kind of core approach to improving a person's ethical conduct that Confucius recommended, in fact.

Buddhist monks, on the other hand, form a new family group – a 'sangha,' within which to enjoy the benefits of teamwork.

Daoists, meanwhile, tend to operate somewhere between those extremes of biological kin and religious community – going with the flow and enjoying taking part in teamwork even when there is only 'mother nature' for company.

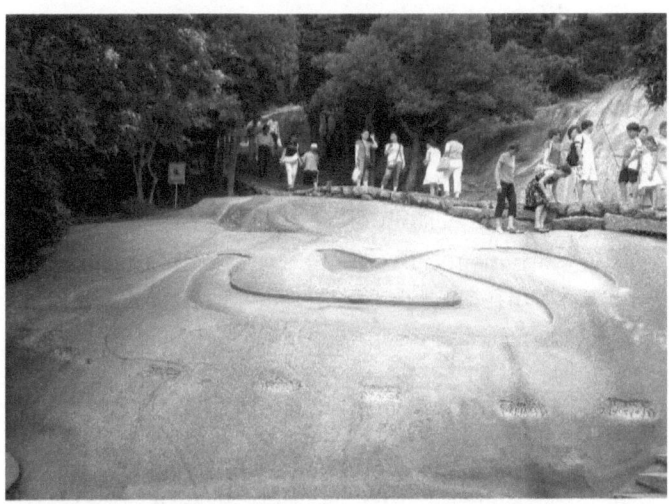

The Chinese character for heart/mind (Xīn – 心) carved into a smooth stone outcrop within a Zen Buddhist temple complex on PuTuo Island in eastern China.

What these approaches all have in common, however – as well as in common with all other major ancient social philosophies, is that they are concerned with *cultivating rewarding virtue*, and thus appreciating warm-heartedness, at all times. For a positive, optimistic, 'can-do' cooperative mindset tends to be the most efficient means of survival when faced with a mostly cold, empty, ever-winding-down universe.

What is more, such civil potential, and the life habits that harness it, also seem to be the primary reason why humans have managed to dominate their planet, and even fly into space, rather than remain limited in their powers in the way that other apes continue to be.

Thus, mindfulness and Zen are ultimately about recognising the wise empowerment that is within reach when one makes the choice to come in from the cold, so to speak – when one decides to nurture one's compassionate heart. And not just by reading books such as this one, but instead through constant *physical practice* within the more abstract yet highly tangible domain of organic being.

Finally, then, and in true Zen tradition, this chapter will finish with a suggestion to the reader to attempt a transcendence of the words contained in this book – so that the real benefit of Zen's wisdom can manifest tangibly and vividly in the world for his or her appreciation, as well as for future generations' sake.

For no matter whether one practices western secular mindfulness, Chinese Zen, yoga, tai chi, Chinese zither, qigong, or whatever other formal mindful art, the teachings of the first patriarch of Zen, Bodhidharma, apply with the same potential power.

This is because all such disciplines point to the same compassionate, prosocial heart that is always available right here, right now – if, that is, we can transcend our obsessions with words and symbols, and expand our bodies and minds in harmony with our natural intent.

Thus, one final time, as stated by the first patriarch of Chinese Zen:

> *"External instructions do not transmit effectively,*
>
> *So therefore do not elevate scriptural doctrines.*
>
> *Just point directly to the human heart,*
>
> *In order to be true Buddha Nature in motion."*

INDEX

A

abdomen, 55, 166
abdominal 'cell', 55
abstract: domain of organic being, 196; ink paintings, 117; qualities, 1; truth, xxxvi, 1, 3, 71, 114, 138, 196
abstruseness, 45, 117
acceptance, 33, 46, 71, 90, 98, 122, 125, 129, 136, 139; *of 'what is'*, 46, 71, 98, 122; of nature, 71
adaptability, 60, 68, 71; fluid, 50, 73
adaptation, 60, 61, 72, 78, 129
adapting, 61, 69, 75, 192
adversity, xi, xv, xxxiii, 35, 40, 45, 47, 51, 52, 59, 64, 68, 78, 86, 126, 192
aggregate selves, 149
aggression, 65, 140
aggressive force, 65
aha moments, 80
aikido, 64, 65
alchemy: internal, 153, 157
Ānāpānasati, 28
anchor, 28
anchoring, 28, 30, 35, 103, 105, 157
anger, 39
animal styles of kung fu, 51
antisociality, 66, 67, 68, 84
anxiety, 39, 162, 163, 170
appetites, 12, 32, 55, 147, 156, 178, 187
archery, iii, iv, v, 175
artistic merit, 90
Assutavā Sutta, 149
asymmetrical universe, 123
asymmetry, 32, 33, 120, 122, 123, 124, 125, 127, 130, 131
athletes, 36
attention: mastering, 30, 39, 40, 51, 58, 75, 113, 117, 123, 133, 145, 147, 166, 171, 193
automatic self-creation, 52
autopoiesis, 52, 53, 56, 71, 75, 76, 112, 192
Awa Kenzo, iv, v
awareness, 18, 31, 53, 82, 86, 156, 157, 159

B

bagua, 151, 152, 157
balance: functional sense of, 131
balancing, 104, 105, 123, 124, 130, 161, 171
ballet, 113
balloons, 54
balls of the feet, 56

bamboo, 50, 51, 52, 59, 115, 116
bamboo style, 94
barbaric activity, 58
become the brush, 99
befriending, 116, 156
being mode, 18
being of service, 169
benevolence, 176, 177
beyond words, 12, 13, 17, 71, 76, 112, 161, 164, 177, 181, 183, 192
big bang, 12, 44
Big Self, 158
binary, 3, 151, 152
biophysical situation, 192
Bodhidharma, 13, 14, 16, 18, 71, 174, 196
Bodhisattva Vow, 169
body language, xiii, 49, 74, 84, 190
body scan, 167
boredom, xvii, 39, 170
boxing, xxxii, xxxiii, xxxiv
branches, 50, 52, 63, 127
breath, 28, 31, 40, 51, 54, 103, 115, 117, 122, 129, 156, 157, 160, 161, 166, 167, 175
breath work, 166
breathing into one's limbs, 166
breathing process, 51, 166
brewing Zen tea, 152, 169
broader community, 194
bronzeware style, 94, 96, 101

Bruce Lee, 73
brush, 88, 93, 94, 96, 99, 101, 111, 184
brush skill, 134
buddha, xix, 37, 44, 49, 77, 164
Buddha, 14, 16, 27, 35, 52, 65, 77, 112, 149, 150, 162, 163, 187, 188, 191, 197
Buddha Nature, 14, 52, 112, 197
buddhahood, xii, 34, 163, 186
Buddhism: Chinese, xxvi, 34, 102, 183; Chinese Zen, 17, 35
Buddhist meditation, xii, 184, 215
busy life, 140

C

CānTóngQì, 154
caring attitude, 48, 49
cellular community, 150
cellular fractal symmetry, 53
cellular springiness, 50, 56
cellular structures, 52, 63
channeling, x, xix, 66, 68
chanting, xii, xviii, xix, 9
chaotic forces, 33
charioteering, 175
Chinese character evolution, 94
choiceless awareness. *See* spacious awareness, *See*

spacious awareness
chores, 16, 147
circulation, 53, 56, 146, 168
civil societies, 41
civil values, xxxii, 39
clarity, 40, 81, 103, 146
Classic of Tea, 141, 150
classical art, 90, 91
classical Chinese literature, 176
cleaning, 31, 144
clouds of dust, 36
co-dependent arising, 160
cognitive emergence, 5
cold-heartedness, 85, 86
collective benefits, 177
combat, 81
compassion, 89, 141, 145, 156, 157, 164, 169, 174, 196
competitiveness, 35, 174, 185
complexes, 30
complexity, 30, 34, 35
composition, 114, 115, 123, 124, 136, 137
compulsion, 50, 157
conatus, 112
Confucian arts, 182
Confucianism, 17, 35, 183, 189
Confucius, xxxvii, 4, 5, 6, 7, 8, 9, 10, 12, 13, 14, 18, 21, 25, 26, 138, 164, 169, 175, 176, 177, 178, 180, 181, 182, 195
congruence, xxi, 14, 31, 33, 37, 39, 54, 59, 68, 75, 76, 86, 103, 169
constant change, 1, 105
cooling down, 97, 173
cooperation, 193
core motifs and textures, 116
correct one's heart, 180
Cratylus, 73, 74
creative intelligence, 66
creative process, 80
cross-pollination, 184
crown of the head, 51, 56
Cui Ruibin, i, xxvi, xxix, xxxii, xxxiii, xxxiv, xxxv, 184
cultivation, 41, 148, 178, 179; personal, xxiv, 89
Cultural Revolution, xxiv
cunning tricks, 65

D

daily practice, xxvii, xxix, xxxi, xxxiv, 16, 31, 38, 40, 64, 69, 75, 86, 89, 123, 130, 131, 143, 144, 147, 170, 174, 184, 186
dance, 31, 76, 87, 89; yiquan 'jianwu', 76
DàoDéJīng, 9, 10, 19, 23, 61, 66, 68, 73, 77, 79
Daoism, 17, 35, 183, 189
Dawkins, Richard, 49, 66, 113
death, vii, xv, xxi, 30, 58, 150, 152, 162, 163, 192
decluttering, 143
deeper beauty, 92

depression, xxix, 32
Deshimaru, Taisen, xx
desire, 10, 115, 174
devil is in the detail, 36, 177
Dhamma, 25, 26, 27
Dhammapada, 65
dhyana, 13
diaphragm, 31, 51, 103
dignity, 39, 112, 116, 136, 146, 169, 175
direct reality, iv, xv, xxxi, 8, 13, 18, 30, 33, 49, 61, 74, 81, 113, 144, 158, 159, 160, 177, 190, 197
discipline, v, vi, xvii, xix, 48, 49, 53, 64, 69, 144, 146, 185, 186; regimen, xxxi, 36, 75
dis-ease, 32, 38, 56, 90, 91
dissociation, 30, 38
doctrinal conflict, 34
doing mode, 18
domestic life, 146, 147
dragon, 68, 70, 72, 76, 82, 83, 104; ball, 82
drama, 174
dysfunction, 30, 49, 123, 124, 131

E

eating, xxxi, 31, 42, 74
economics, 12, 67, 71, 122, 169, 176, 177, 178, 181, 182, 194; basic activity, 177; Confucian rewards, 181; prosocial, 193

effort, xxxi, 37, 38, 86, 96
effortlessness, 64, 75, 86, 117, 170
ego, 37, 45, 77, 84, 115
eight week mindfulness course, xxviii, xxxvi, 215
Eightfold Path, 29
elasticity, 50, 51
elegance, xxxvi, 60, 71, 75, 89, 147
elements: Chinese five, 150, 151, 153, 157, 161, 162; qualities (Buddhism), 150
elongation, 54
empowerment, xxxiv, xxxv, 55, 81, 85, 92, 130, 140, 186, 192, 196
emptiness, 2, 26, 28, 44, 45, 46, 47, 50, 61, 79, 80, 81, 82, 83, 84, 85, 114, 123, 139, 143, 156, 158, 159, 196
energy: efficient use, 175; electrochemical, 165; fresher, 166; habit, 156
engaged: Buddhism, 194; prosociality, 41
enlightenment, xviii, 38, 44, 49, 61, 139, 144, 186, 191; inherent, 52; state, 38
equanimity, 41, 89
etiquette, 146, 169
eudaimonia, 37
euphoria, 55
evolution, 41, 60

excelling, 40
exercising, xix, 31
existence: effortless, 32; existential condition, 45; natural, 31; nature of, 38; nourishing, 171; optimised, 71; purpose and origin, 189; seamless, 96, 164
existential urgency, 39
expansion, xxxiii, 55, 58, 104, 171
explosive power, xxxii, 60
explosive strikes, 57

F

failing one's way to success, 126
faith, xii, xv, xxii, 31, 85, 112
Faith in Mind Inscription, 15
family, ix, xx, xxii, xxiii, 47, 143, 175, 177, 193, 194, 195
feet to hands, xxxii, xxxiii
fencing, xxxii
Finding Flow, 37
fine movements, 90
fine skill, 35, 105
finer life, xv, 36, 78, 166, 173
fish, 40
flexibility, xxxi, 46, 50, 52, 59, 60, 68, 100
flinching, 56
flow, xv, 12, 18, 29, 31, 36, 37, 38, 39, 41, 42, 47, 59, 78, 85, 86, 90, 105, 117, 130, 133, 137, 139, 144, 152, 156, 159, 160, 167, 170, 171, 184, 187, 189; state, 38, 170
flowing, xiv, xix, 27, 30, 31, 37, 38, 40, 61, 66, 73, 75, 76, 77, 85, 86, 89, 90, 96, 97, 100, 106, 110, 115, 123, 134, 148, 157, 164, 165, 169, 171; in harmony, 38, 61, 77, 106, 171; warrior, 86
fluid expansiveness, 60
fluidity, xxxi, 26, 41, 47, 50, 58, 60, 66, 70, 71, 73, 76, 77, 78, 81, 84, 85, 90, 94, 96, 103, 104, 167, 170; of 'what is', 74; socio-economic, 66
fluidity of being, 60
flying white, 114
follow your heart, xxiii
form is emptiness, and emptiness is form, 158
formalities, 169
formlessness, 43, 46, 47, 49, 51, 53, 61, 76
forms: absolute, 45, 139; mental, 49; potent, 158; prescribed, 43, 54; rigid, 44, 45, 47, 60, 74
four arts of the scholarly gentleman, 176, 182
four noble truths, 188
friction with air, 184
frolicking, 76, 106

from heart to hand, 99
fullness of being, 53

G

gardens, 133; royal, 124; Zen, 133
genetic selfishness, 49
'get in the groove', 9, 36, 161
global inheritance, 187
glory in victory, 58
go (board game), 176
go have some tea, 144
go with the flow, 167
going forth into thusness, 71
Golden Rule, 41
graceful movements, 31
grass, 51
Great Determination, 39
Great Learning, 178
Greco-Buddhism, 186
Greek culture, 24, 26, 73, 90, 186
green tea, xxvi, 113, 144, 145
growth (organic), 79
Guānyīn, xii
guns, xxxii

H

habits, 174; civil, 196
hara, 55
hard work, vi, 59, 91
harmony, 168; with the now, 37
harnessing nature, 98
Heart Sutra, xii, xiii, xviii, 71, 158
heavens and earth, 10, 11, 12, 16
Heidegger, 12
Heraclitus, 24, 25, 26, 73, 74
Herrigel, iii, iv, v, vi
hexagrams, 3
hiking, 139, 140
hot water, 170
human condition, 2, 6, 14, 38, 116, 136, 162, 186
Hume, David, 1
humility, xxv, 100, 140, 168
hydration, 142
hygiene ritual, 142

I

I-Ching, 2, 3, 5, 6, 151, 152
identity, 150; permanent, 139
ignorance, 92, 125, 174
image weighting, 123
immortality, 149, 159, 163; fantasy, 30
imperfections, 30
impermanence, xxxiii, 26, 27, 45, 46, 47, 61, 69, 71, 73, 74, 76, 77, 85, 105, 139, 150, 163, 170
impersonal, 5, 31, 44, 115, 116, 158, 159, 170
impersonal flow, 29
impersonality, 164
impurity, 124
individuality: absolute, 160
individuals, 32, 130, 175,

176, 187
infinite Way, 186
inherent autopoietic agenda, 54
ink: drunken, 129; shades and effects, 114; textures, 114, 134
intelligence: inherent, 44, 52; reflexive, 44, 80
intent, xvi, 50, 51, 54, 58, 59, 61, 96, 111, 115, 117, 127, 134, 145, 169, 181, 197; efficient survival, 181; universal dynamic, 115
intention, vi, 17, 50, 52, 53, 56, 61, 69, 76, 84, 92, 99, 112, 113, 142, 143, 145, 147, 148, 175, 180, 184, 192; civil, 182
International Yiquan Academy, i, xxvi, xxix
intoxication, 56
intra-cellular cohesion, 65
iron shirt, 56

J

Japan, iii, iv, v, vi, xx, xxii, xxv, 35, 127, 129, 164
Jasmine Zhang, i, xxv, 183, 184
Journey to the West, ix, xii, xviii, 162

K

Kabat-Zinn, Jon, xxvii, 48, 65
Kailash, Mt., 137
kendo, xx
kintsugi, 130
knee pain, xviii, xxxiv
knees, xxiii
koan, 82, 144
kyūdō, iii, iv, v

L

labelling, 25
Laṅkāvatāra Sūtra, 16
LaoTzu, 9, 10, 11, 12, 13, 14, 19, 21, 23, 25, 26, 61, 66, 68, 73, 77, 79, 164, 177, 178
large states, 178
laws: cosmic, 178; of impermanence, 26, 47; of nature, 18, 25, 30, 177, 180; of the heavens, 24, 191; of the heavens and the earth, 191; socioeconomic, 177
Leibniz, 152
letting go, xviii, 29, 30, 54, 61, 80, 82, 86, 112, 160, 161
liberation, 27, 76, 187
lifestyle: assets, 183; broadly functional, 194; ethics-driven, 178
literati, 110
log, 46, 77

Logos, 25, 27
loss, 31, 47, 69, 71, 98, 120, 162
lotus posture, 52
loving kindness, 66, 174
LuYu, 141, 143, 144, 150, 152, 156, 157, 158, 159, 161, 162, 164

M

Mahāparinibbāṇa Sutta, 27
mania, xxxi, 39, 173
Manjushri, 102, 103
many hands make lighter work, 41, 67, 177
marriage, 32
massage, 31, 56, 64, 82, 166
mastery, xviii, xxxii, xxxiii, 9, 185
mathematics, 151, 175
MBSR, xxviii, xxxvi
melting, 86, 101, 102, 168
membranes, 50, 51, 60
memes, 49
memorising, 8, 9, 91
mental gymnastics, 28, 159
mental illness, 32
metabolism, 55, 75
metaphysical beliefs, 187
mind: abstractions of, 149; as body, 161; autopoietic, 78; everyday, 170; judgmental, 105; natural, 76; refresh, 143; sword, 103; universal, 170
mind stream, xix, 9

mindfulness: 'revolution', 33, 125
mindfulness 'revolution', xxviii
misfortune, 32, 33, 131
mixed martial arts, xi, 35, 190
MMA. *See* mixed martial arts
momentum: one spirited, 77; wholesome, 29
monasteries, 143, 144
monastic practice, 143
Mongol invasions, 33
monkey king, x, xiv, xviii, 162, 163
monkey mind, 162
monks, xxvi, 9, 13, 35, 119, 127, 143, 144, 195
mortality, 69, 149
mother nature, 178
mountain and water paintings, 134, 138
mundane life, 16, 38, 147, 170
music, 5, 31, 113, 175
mutations, 60
mutual service, 170

N

name it and claim it, 12
natural environment, 50
natural phases, 3
natural scenery, 110
nature: chaotic, 129; creative heart of, 137; harmony with, 185; immersion,

184; inherent asymmetry, 127; investigating, 179, 180; relationship with, 88; seamless, 159; spending time in, 109
Nietzsche, 90, 130
ninja, xi, xii, xiii, xviii
no death, 163
no self-deception, 178
Noble Eightfold Path, 28
non-grasping, 76
non-temporality, 38
novelty, 45, 47, 127, 162

O

On Nature, 25
one's own unique Way., 27
Oneness, 37, 38, 171
openness, 71
opportunism, 66
optimism, vii, 39, 70, 185
oracle bone style, 94, 96, 101
organic: beauty, 75, 124; shapes, 94, 184; truths, 30

P

parasitism, 67, 194
passage of time, 37
passion, xxxi, 174
path, xvii, xxxiii, xxxvii, 8, 17, 26, 39, 42, 57, 65, 88, 92, 98, 125, 139, 143, 144, 162, 170, 174, 183; of the warrior, 65

Paul Wang, i, xxv, 183, 184
peace: inner, 32, 33, 41, 42, 87, 140, 175
peaceful ethics, 41
peaceful heart, xxxi, 31, 38, 39, 41, 55, 74, 78, 87, 89, 97, 98, 115, 136, 156, 171, 174, 178
Persian culture, 186
persistence, xvi, 185, 186
persisting, xvii, 39, 48, 50, 61, 63
philosophy: Chinese traditional competing, 35; communal, 41; of pure presence, 63; practical, xv, xxxvii, 6, 17, 32, 67, 73, 94; Zen, v, xvi, 38
pine, 50, 52, 126, 127
plants, 50, 110, 121, 122, 133, 184, 193
poetry, 113, 183
politeness, 41, 146, 169, 193
PōMò. *See* splashed ink painting
post-natal condition, 167
posture: perfect, 44; stationary, 48, 49
potency, xxxi, xxxiii, 61, 68, 69, 164, 169
power lines (boxing), xxxii
predisposition, 75, 169, 193
pressure, xix, xxxiii, xxxiv, 46, 50, 64, 84
pressure testing, 46
productivity, 79

propaganda: of depression, 32; of the ego, 65, 102
proselytising, 169
psychological freedoms, 189
psychological landscapes, 138
pure action, 16
pure feeling, 37
pure physical nature, 112
push-hands, xxx, xxxi, xxxiv, 35, 48, 63, 64, 69, 74, 81, 82, 84, 92

Q

qigong, xxiv, 156, 165, 166, 167, 183, 184, 196
Qīngyuán Wéixìn, 139

R

receptiveness, 81, 82, 84
red in tooth and claw, 66
reframing, xxvii, 32, 125
regrets, 193
rehabilitation, 47, 48
resilience, 53, 54, 56, 57, 59, 66, 129, 192; inner, 58
responsibility, xxxvi, 66, 170, 178
restrictive cultural trends, 49
Right Concentration, 28, 29
Right Mindfulness, 28, 29
rigid belief systems, 32
rigid concepts, 61
ritual, xxvi, 5, 41, 146, 147, 174
rolling with the punches, 47, 74
rooting, xvi, xxviii, 34, 45, 50, 56, 57, 59, 63, 64, 82, 84, 149, 182
routine, 31, 144, 145

S

samurai, xx, 35
sanda, xxxiii
Satipatthāna Sutta, 150
schedule, xxvi, 88, 144
scientific community, xxvii, xxviii
seasons, 1, 7, 25, 39, 152; of the heart, 39
seated meditation, xxix, 75, 113, 169
seated Zen, xviii, xx, xxvi, xxvii, 52, 64
secular mindfulness, xxvi, xxvii, xxviii, xxix, xxx, xxxvi, xxxvii, 17, 28, 29, 33, 36, 42, 52, 53, 58, 65, 103, 112, 120, 125, 130, 160, 167, 180, 183, 184, 187, 189, 196, 215
self: aggregate, 82, 149, 150, 163; bundle theory, 150, 158; permanent, 159; physical, 150, 163
self-compassion, 49, 145, 147
self-ishness, 44, 85
sense of brush, 104
sense of friction, 103, 105

shallow symbols, xvi, 18
Shaolin kung fu, 43, 71
Shaolin Temple, 35, 190
shifting attention, 39
sincerity, 22, 181
six arts of the perfect gentleman, 175, 176, 182
small states, 178
snake, 57, 58, 68, 86
social contract, 170
social environments, 124
socialising, 31, 37
softness, 85
Sōtō Zen, xviii, xx, xxviii, 44, 55, 88, 158, 173
soul, 25, 149
spacious awareness, 28, 53, 138; via calligraphy, 88; via painting, 53, 115, 117, 161; via tea ceremony, 159, 164; via yiquan, 61
sparring, xxxi, 92
speaking, 7, 31, 41, 123
spine, xvii, 32, 51, 82
spirit, vi, x, xxiii, 13, 37, 51, 52, 53, 59, 65, 77, 90, 94, 95, 96, 99, 101, 111, 115, 127, 136, 137, 162, 166, 170, 184, 185, 187
spirit of repetition, 185
spiritual, xxvi, 33, 35, 41, 76, 92, 101, 104, 113, 115, 137, 138, 140, 162, 174, 182
spiritual flame, 102, 159
splashed ink painting, 127

spontaneity: creativity, 47; maintained, 89
sport, xxxii, xxxiii, 58
springy sensations, 51
stagnation, 165, 166
stance: resilient, 44, 46; self-compassion, 49
standing, x, xvii, xxiv, xxx, xxxiv, xxxv, 48, 50, 55, 59, 64, 75
storms, 47, 64, 74, 106
stream of consciousness, 78, 169
strength-enhancement, 48
stun tactics, 56
subconscious, 17, 39, 54, 146
subtleties, xvi, xxxvi, 10, 11, 29, 36, 38, 50, 51, 88, 173, 177; obscurity, 25, 76
SunTzu, 81
surrendering, 45, 78, 84, 92, 100, 103, 104, 114, 136
survival, 41, 49, 60, 176, 183, 196
sustained progress, 39
Suzuki, Shunryu, 44, 60, 88, 158, 173, 185
swimming, 40, 76
swords, xviii, xx, xxiv, 101, 102, 103, 104; ninja, xii

T

taekwondo, xiii
tai chi, xiii, xvi, xxi, xxiv, xxv, 35, 55, 56, 64, 73, 90,

104, 113, 120, 167, 183, 196
tangible wisdom, 196
Tao Teh Ching. *See* DàoDéJīng
Taoism. *See* Daoism
tea and Zen one flavour, 164
tea ceremony, 142, 158, 159, 169
tea saint. *See* LuYu
teamwork, 177, 195
tension, 168
Thales of Miletus, 73
The Analects, 6, 8, 18, 138
The Art of War, 81
The Confucian Book of Rites, 21, 179
the divine, 37
the good life, 37
The Selfish Gene, 49, 66, 113
the void, 175
Thich Nhat Hanh, 130, 156, 158, 194
thoughts, 82, 112, 113, 122, 129, 181, 192
Tibetan Buddhism, 33, 34, 137
tigers, 51, 70
tough and assertive, 58
tough yet flexible, 50, 59
toughness, 56
traditional Chinese medicine, 150, 151, 165, 184
trance, 83
transcendence, xiv, xvi, 10, 14, 32, 35, 36, 49, 54, 92, 98, 110, 116, 139, 161, 190, 196
trees, i, 50, 51, 52, 56, 59, 75, 126, 127, 184
trial by combat, 35
trigram: fire, 151, 152, 156; water, 151, 152, 156; wind, 151, 152, 156
true yiquan, 54
truth: absolute, 164; bitter, 45; direct, 14; fluid, 85; of nature, xv, 25, 74, 139, 191; organic, 30; practical, xxxi, 84, 122; sincere, 180; true nature, vi, 5, 37, 38, 44, 49, 75, 76, 77, 81, 84, 96, 97, 117, 127, 148, 152, 159, 160, 168, 170, 189; ugly, 92; ultimate, 14
tuning oneself, 24, 31, 51, 54, 55, 75, 76, 77, 96
turbulence, 35, 40
twisting the brush, 89

U

uncluttered view, 79
uneducated humans, 58
unified culture, 183
upright seated posture, 146

V

Vedic culture, 52
vices, 174
victory, 65, 78, 85, 86

Vimalakīrti Sūtra, 16
violence, 32, 41, 58, 66
virtue, 3, 8, 14, 137, 138, 176, 179, 194; cultivating, 195; kingly, 177
virtuous heart, 14

W

Wáng Xiāngzhāi, 48
Wáng Xīzhī, 94, 95
WángMò, 127
warrior sage, 85
water, xxv, 55, 56, 61, 73, 77, 78, 87, 94, 112, 117, 120, 122, 123, 133, 134, 136, 137, 138, 139, 141, 142, 143, 145, 147, 148, 150, 152, 156, 157, 159, 165, 168, 170, 171; profound element, 142
Way of the First Kings, 176
Way of the heavens, 21, 177
weapon, xxxi, 46, 81, 104
weapons, xiii, xxxi, 56
western culture, 124
western landscape painting, 134
'what is': honouring, 193; tangible laws of the heavens, 24
whole body cellularity, 54
whole body intra-connectivity, 57
wholesome vigour, 50
wind stove, 150, 152, 161
winds of human fortune, 187
wingchun kung fu, xiii, xvi
winning, 23, 45, 84
win-win cooperative strategies, 176, 177, 182
wisdom: Way, 183
wooden post. *See* ZhànZhuāng
written paintings, 110, 111
WuWei, 18, 19

X

XiěYìGuóHuà, 111
xingyiquan, 43
XìnXīn Míng. *See* Faith in Mind Inscription

Y

Yì, 9, 21, 50, 51, 56, 96, 99, 111, 180, 181, 182, 184
YìJīng. *See* I-Ching
yin-yang, 35, 97, 123, 124, 138, 151
yiquan posture training, 44, 55
yoga, xxiii, xxxiv, 48, 52, 53, 69, 120, 153, 183, 196
Yú YǒngNián, 48

Z

zazen, xviii, 44, 51, 55, 76
Zen battle, 66
Zen bullshit, 28
Zen mountain, xx
Zen patriarchs, 34

Zen riddle. *See* koan
zendo, xviii, xx, xxii
Zhan Zhuang & the Search of Wu, 48
ZhànZhuāng, xvii
Zhàozhōu Cóngshěn, 143
zither, 196

ABOUT THE AUTHOR

Tristan Petts is a British teacher and artist who has spent almost a third of his life living and working in China. His practice of mindful arts and formal meditation spans more than twenty years, involving Buddhist meditation retreats, attending and completing a standard secular eight week Mindfulness-Based Cognitive Therapy (MBCT) course, attending and completing MBCT instructor training in the United Kingdom, practicing and teaching various martial arts disciplines, as well as traditional Chinese calligraphy, painting, and informal zen tea ceremonies.

Tristan holds a university diploma in counselling skills and theory, and has studied and practiced western secular mindfulness meditation alongside traditional Chinese Zen arts for more than a decade.

As well as having successfully facilitated a number of standard eight-week mindfulness courses, he has also held weekly secular mindfulness walk-in sessions for groups of various sizes.

www.ingramcontent.com/pod-product-compliance
Lightning Source LLC
Chambersburg PA
CBHW031613210526
45464CB00004B/1553